How an Atlanta Contractor Can Grow To $2,000,000 With a Six-Figure Net.

By Jemel Smith CFO

Profit and Growth Expert
Go.Bottomline.tax/contractors

Table of contents

| FORWARD:

If you want to grow your Atlanta construction or building trades business to two million or more, please read the forward first. It will explain why I wrote this book expressly for the 18,195 contractors in the Atlanta metropolitan area.

It is for the local firms that want to accumulate generational wealth by scraping 20% of the gross revenue off the top as net income, living on as little as possible, and investing the balance. Then in the future to sell the business for five times profit.

Now, some of you would like to build a $5-million or $10-million a year business. The secret is to lay the groundwork as you grow to two and then simply wash, rinse, and repeat.

At $2-million, you have the cash flow and gravitas to hire the right managers. Those managers will take the chaos out of your life. That is why you'll work fewer hours and finally have the sleep of the Angels. Even better, your income will deliver the dreams you have for your family.

So, how hard is it to get to the next level? A lot easier than you might imagine. For example: if you are running a business doing $500,000 a year in revenue.

All you need to do is

- Increase the number of new projects by 1.5% a month
- Increase your' bid/won' ratio by 1.5% a month
- Increase the size of the projects you take on by 1.5% a month

The compound effect of small incremental improvements, in this case, would move you from $500,000 per year to $7,000,000 per year in sixty months. That is only five years from now. So, using this as a formula gives you a clear path to 2 million in 24 to 36 months.

CAUTION: The formula is simple; the devil is in the details. Making small incremental improvements will only happen if you are running a tight ship. With the right team in place, you will make it happen.

Right now, Atlanta is in a building boom that will continue as business people migrate to Georgia. We are in a building a boom like none we have ever seen. You are in a rare opportunity (some might say once in a lifetime) to move your construction business to the next level.

A company doing two, five, or even ten million will create generational wealth for your family. It will allow you the opportunity to contribute to your community. You will impact hundreds of employees who will learn from you. Your customers will enjoy the 'builds' you create for years to come. You are in service to others, and because of that, you will enjoy the financial and emotional rewards.

However, there are dangers in taking on more employees and bidding for bigger jobs that will put your future at risk. In this book, we will talk about that risk.

In the average size construction business, the owner can operate like a rugged individualist. We know that is a Georgia tradition; we all feel like we must be in charge of everything that happens. But 'rugged' has limits. Somewhere between $500,000 to $1,000,000 a year in revenue, your control over events starts to slip. You can no longer keep up with every employee, customer, and vendor. You start spinning your wheels. If you are up to working 50 and 60 hours a week, it may already be happening. If you are up at night worrying about a hundred details that you may have overlooked, it probably is happening. If your cash flow stinks – there should be no doubt – you're losing control.

Other contractors have had the same problems. In this book, you will find the strategic steps that every two to ten-million-plus company in Georgia took to get where they are. The list is daunting, but you do not need to do it alone, and you do not need to get it all done today. When I was impatient as a child, my mother would tell me "God invented time, so everything does not happen at once."

I hope to show you why you must start doing less, not more, if you want to create wealth and a lifestyle. Doing less becomes a lot easier at $2-million in revenue.

You are about to read a series of stories about other contractors that I have worked with and how they suffered from frustration to the point of thinking about giving up. That was until they discovered that somebody else had solved the same problems you are facing, and it is okay to borrow their answers. Other contractors discovered that most of their problems were caused by accepting bad jobs, keeping chaotic employees on payroll way too long, and doing work for unreasonable customers.

They learned that financial success comes from repeat orders from good buyers, and new customers should be coming in as referrals. Over the next hour or so, you will realize how important it is to hire competent management in finance, production, and marketing to take the daily grind away from the owner. But hiring must be done systematically as your cash flow grows from bigger and better jobs.

On top of all that, my greatest hope for you is that you discover 'your numbers.' The secret to sleeping at night is running the business using your accounting software reports. You must trust and understand what your numbers mean so you can make the right decisions. It may be hard to imagine, but 80% to 90% of what you need to know to build a better business is hiding in your accounting software.

Running a construction business at a half-million dollars a year is not that hard, but it is a lot of hours. However, growing past that point is a ruthless job until you get to $2-million. That is because you will suffer growing pains as you learn how to be a business owner at a whole new level. Your job description will change as you grow.

I arranged the stories in this book in order of what you should work on first and what comes next. It is a roadmap to get to $2-million in annual revenue (and beyond).

Read this book if you are looking for a proven plan to work fewer hours and have the income you want. You will find that map through the successes and failures of other Atlanta contractors like you. Read this book if you want to have a company that makes you proud. Read this book if you want to make a bigger and more positive impact on your community.

One last word: my favorite prayer that I discovered way too late in life is simple: "Lord, may what I have be enough." The purpose of life is to serve others, not to get rich. However, the more you serve those around you, the more the world rewards you. Focus on your family, your employees, and then your customer; in turn, they will help you reach your dreams.

Let's get started.

Jemel Smith

Bottom Line Tax Services LLC

Douglasville Georgia

CHAPTER 1:
THE HOUSEWIFE STOOD BY THE ELEVATOR, CRYING

The QuickBooks for contractors training class I was leading was going well, and it was time for a break. I left some worksheets in the truck, so I headed for the hotel elevator while the bookkeepers and wives of contractors headed for the cookies my family baked the night before.

Down the hall, I saw a young woman standing in the corner crying. I recognized her as the wallflower sitting in the back of the class who had not asked a single question in the first hour, and here she was bawling her eyes out. Of course, I had to ask why. I would be a cold-hearted bean counter if I did not.

As she spun around, "Janet" started telling me about the fight she had with her husband "Randy" at the breakfast table that morning. For the past two years, she had been doing the books for their electrical contracting business.

Janet had no idea how to do bookkeeping, but was determined to help her family any way she could because it was important to her husband to be his own boss. She had read everything she could on accounting, even that big yellow book called *Bookkeeping for Dummies*. For months, she held a newborn in one arm and a QuickBooks manual in the other. None of it made sense, and after one hour in my class, it was worse.

Janet's two-year struggle culminated in a bad argument that morning. It seems that on the previous Friday, Randy had picked up a $25,000 deposit to start the next job. The biggest they'd ever done.

At breakfast, he talked about buying a new generator. "The one I need is on sale for $1,299," he told her. Then Janet blurted out: "We cannot afford it. I used that $25,000 to pay off the overdue bills from the last job. Elliot's Supply has called me three times."

Randy slammed down his coffee cup and started showing the kids why they called him "Sparky" down at the job site. The fight ended when he stormed out the door and spun gravel across the yard as he drove away.

I looked at her crying, shaking, feeling like it was her fault, and I realized that if this kept up, those three kids at the breakfast table were only going to see their father every other weekend. I knew then that I had to show this couple how they could have everything they wanted for their family, and it would be easier than they thought.

Over the past twenty years, I observed the Janet and Randy story play out dozens of times with the same sad ending. The business closes, sometimes the family dissolves, and any hope of making the big-time fades into the west Georgia sunset. Construction is a competitive business, and you need to run it like a tight ship, or you will never stop working yourself to death while your employees take home better paychecks than you.

At the same time, construction is a great business, especially in Georgia, and as I write this book, it looks like it will stay good for at least another five years. Right now, you are looking at a brief window in time where you can line up everything in your favor. The Atlanta construction market has not been this strong for as long as I can remember. Money is almost free; businesses are moving here left and right.

Now is the time to get your ducks in a row, get your finances in order, and get your team in place. You do not see opportunities like this every day. It is time to rock 'n' roll.

When I saw Janet crying, I knew exactly why her husband blew up this morning. I also knew (from watching my other contractors over the past two decades) what she had to do next to save the business and maybe even her marriage.

I thought to myself, "If Randy could talk to someone a few hours a month instead of trying to be a rugged individualist, he would be on his way to the 1%, not yelling at his wife." He was landing jobs, but he did not know how to get the chaos out of his business, so he and his family would enjoy positive cash flow and peace at home.

KEY IDEA:

What is the 1%, and why is it important? If your income hits $400,000, you make more than 99% of the people in America, but it is only a number I use to help my clients understand how they are doing.

You may be happy with less, but it is easier to understand the lessons if we tie them to empirical evidence. Saying "I want to be rich" or "I want to be happy in my business" is not a goal; it is a wish. Wishes are challenging to build a plan around.

CHAPTER 2:
HOW TO GET YOUR FIRM TO $2-MILLION IN REVENUE, AND WHY THAT SHOULD BE YOUR GOAL

I knew from experience that business owners like Janet and Randy needed to get their company to $2-million in annual revenue; at that point, the cash flow would be enough to push everything into place.

But you will not get to $2-million if you do not have your ducks in a row. In Dallas, some guy named Mark Cuban loves to say, "Sales will solve all problems." Well, all I can say is "bless his heart" because what he did not tell you is a business that does not have their finances in order first will never get a chance to hit the "sales solve all problems" level.

Before Randy ever gets to $2-million, too many things will go wrong because he will suffer from the sin of 'inaccurate assumptions' and make poor decisions, many of them repeatedly. The poorly run operation will bust out long before it ever smooths out.

All accountants have that moment when they think, "If this client only knew what I know about running a business, they would be rich by now."

So, standing by the elevator with a crying homemaker, I committed to sharing a string of stories about other contractors and how they solved problems that we all have. Owning a business is a never-ending flood of problems. But as Tony Soprano used to say, "It's the life we chose."

So, I am hoping the next Janet and Randy will take an hour to learn from the successes and failures of other Atlanta contractors by reading this book. A business is a lot of fun when you don't have to suffer through the chaos.

Two Key Takeaways from This Book That Will Make Your Life Easier

1. Every construction business has one or two types of projects that they are great at building. Even more important, we all have a type of customer we call the "good client." If you can figure out what that build is and who you like as a customer, you can focus on doing more of that one thing. As a result, your reputation, referrals, repeat business, annual revenue, and net profit will skyrocket over the next few years.

2. Every one of us has customers, jobs, employees, bankers, and vendors that create chaos. They are sucking the life out of you. If you can isolate the person or problem interrupting your workflow, you can remove the confusion. Successful business owners in the 1% are the happiest people I know, and I hope you can join their ranks from what you learn here.

The simple way to understand all this is to start with something you already know: the 80/20 rule.

It means that 20% of what you do in your business drives 80% of your net income. At the same time, 80% of what you do is an emotional drain and a waste of time. Sorting out the good, the bad, and the ugly is critical if you want more fun in your business, and remember, people who have fun make money.

In my work as a part-time contract CFO for Atlanta area construction companies, my clients keep the go, and I take the bad and the ugly out behind the woodshed.

Who Am I? Do I Know Construction?

My name is Jemel Smith. I founded Bottom Line Tax because I saw how my family struggled with the taxes, profits, and cash flow in their construction business, and I wanted to help.

For 21 years, I have worked with contractors to help them understand their numbers. There are no examples of a contractor getting to the next level while ignoring their numbers, and that's because the secrets of our future success are buried in our accounting software.

Oh, and by the way, I am not a CPA. Here is why. CPAs spend most of their time understanding GAP rules for publicly traded companies. I found my clients far more interested in knowing how to control cost, bid for better jobs and keep the tax bills as low as possible. These are lessons learned on the ground, not in Harvard.

As for my focus on construction, it is almost all I do. I get great satisfaction from helping a business owner who can look at a worn-out kitchen and see gourmet dinners for eight friends next month. Someone who can see a brush-covered piece of hilly dirt and think about kids playing in the backyard pool this time next year. I enjoy honest, hardworking visionaries who are building a better Georgia. This is my home, and I want to see it continue to be the best place to raise a family in the world.

In this book, you will read stories about builders on their way to $2-million and some headed to $10-million. These stories are all taken from my years of working for Atlanta contractors as a part-time CFO.

These are people you have seen at the lumber yard or talked to at the truck show. You may have even bid against them (and probably lost). So, for privacy's sake, I have switched the names and details.

The state of Georgia is serious about its code of conduct – what I hear in my office stays in my office. But these are real-life stories that you can learn from, and they are going to help your business and life get a lot better.

Why $2-Million?

Over the years, I discovered that $2-million seems to be the number where you have enough revenue to move chaos out of your life.

You can bid on better jobs at that level because you can afford a top-notch crew that shares your vision. You can attract loyal employees who will retire from your business in thirty years with a good pension. And your business can turn into a cash cow for you.

However, those are not the most important reasons for getting to $2-million. The more success you have in your business, the more positive choices you can make in your life.

The best choice you can make on day one is to start removing friction points and chaos. That is what rich people know that most builders do not understand. Chaos kills our spirit and our wealth. But you can get rid of chaos if you follow the trail other contractors have forged ahead of you. Getting rid of what you do not want to do is the fastest way to get to what you do want to do.

Almost as nice: at $2,000,000, you worry less about the customer who wants a lower-priced bid because you heard the warning signals upfront, and you can walk away. The customer who buys on price is an orange Homer bucket full of future problems. Let's get to the point where you do not need to take those bad jobs because you need the money to make payroll.

At $2-million, you will not need to work so many hours; your kids will not grow up wondering where Daddy is. You will sleep better at night.

Is $2-million even possible?

Yes, and to illustrate how, I like to break down all goals into bite-sized pieces.

Two million dollars is:

- 500-backyard decks
- 200-bathroom remodels
- 100-kitchens
- 7-track houses
- 2-luxury homes
- 1- government contract

> **HUMAN ENGINEERING TIP:** Keep in mind that when you have 500 deck customers, your chances for running into difficult people go off the charts.

Oh, you will get some crazy people; you will meet a few in this book. But the deck builder will find that out of 500 decks, 50 will be failures (10% of clients will hate the job you do, or something is going to go wrong and eat up your profits) which is a huge emotional drain, so you should consider this as you uncover the right path for your business in this book. Decks are easier to sell but harder to deliver.

Let Us Jump Ahead Two to Five Years

Let's say you have followed the steps in this book and hit the $2-million a year threshold, with 20% falling to the bottom line. You did it.

What is next?

At this point, your lifestyle is slowly upgrading because you are in the 1% income earner bracket. You can move your monthly salary to the $15,000 mark and still put $20,000 monthly profit into your pensions and investments.

You could probably cut back to 30 hours a week if you wanted to. You would not need to build a giant cash balance inside your company because the bank will fund your deals.

Now, you can afford that F-350 and the 32-foot cruiser. You might even start looking for that 2nd home out on Lake Lanier. (But only if you could rent it from time to time on VRBO, so it was an investment.)

> **TAX TIP:** Own your cabin in a separate LLC and have your company meetings there. Your corporation can pay the cabin's LLC rent, and the income flows back to you without Social Security taxes at the end of the year.

The day you hit $2-million; I would tell you to take one month off work with two objectives:

1. Come back to work in a month and find out if your business can run without you? If you laid the groundwork properly, you would come back to a company free of chaos. Everything would be as it was on the day you left or better. The month off is a perfect test to determine if you are ready for the next level. Get out of town, so you do not feel tempted to "stop in at the shop" to see how they are doing. Getaway and celebrate.

2. I also recommend you have a serious conversation with your wife about what to do next: "Do we stay at $2-million, or should we go for the next milestone of 5 or 10 million? "Rich people have choices, and either decision is honorable.

I wrote this book knowing that if you follow the processes I have watched other contractors use over 20 years, you will be in the 1% in the next two to three years.

How fast you get there is up to you. There is plenty of work in Atlanta, so sales are going to be easy. Heck, the whole goal is a lot easier than you think.

Can You Do It? Can You Get Your Construction Business to $2-million?

Yes, if you can learn how to be a better business person. At some point, you will step away from the daily tasks and move into the manager's role.

In Atlanta, there are roughly 18,000 construction and building trades businesses. The number is going up every day, so who knows for sure. Of those, about 25% have already gone past the two million mark – others are doing it, you can join them.

It does not matter what area of construction or building trade you are in because somebody has already proven that you can have a much easier life with only a few changes in how you run your operation.

The old saying is, "If one man can do it – so can another." I wrote this book to show you what the big dogs know that you do not.

A successful contractor has learned three skills that make all the difference. No one promotes these skills; you must take the initiative to learn them on your own.

- Your ability to motivate vendors, customers, and employees to move forward with your vision of what they can accomplish. What we call 'human engineering.'

- The business processes you have made an intricate part of your operation, including cash management. What we call 'how we do it here.'

- The team you build. Well, that is simply, team.

Let's cover these in a little more detail.

1. HUMAN ENGINEERING: Success in construction, like any business, boils down to your skill in getting people to follow your vision and contribute to the best of their ability. Each person you write a check to or who writes a check to you is a human being.

Since a human is behind every movement of money in your life, you must understand their fears, wants, and desires. Human engineering lets you sell better jobs at higher prices and helps you motivate your team to pull the wagon together.

Human engineering is a learned art. Nobody is born "good" at managing people. With a systematic plan, you can build a great team of people who want to be part of your vision. You will attract the best customers.

2. HOW WE DO IT: The most successful contractors figure out what they are good at early on. They know the one thing they do where almost no one else can come close. They have learned to focus all their energy on that ONE THING. They put all their eggs in that one basket, and then they watch the damn basket.

If you focused on doing less, you would have less chaos in your life. You would develop checklists, pre-written rules for dealing with the exceptions, and a team of experienced tradesmen to handle most problems.

Unfortunately, this does not happen overnight. Most contractors end up writing business rules and processes after something gets screwed up. That is fine; trying to plan for every contingency will make you crazy. Fixing problems (once and for all) can be done as you go.

IMPORTANT: Financial controls are part of the business process. Without a solid understanding of how you did today, you will make inaccurate assumptions on what to do tomorrow. Remember that a lean dog runs fast.

Your reputation for delivering that "one" type of build will grow, and you will achieve more referrals and receive better prices for your work. If you have read about Bezos, Musk, Gates, or Buffett, they all use the word "FOCUS" to describe why and how they did so well.

But what about marketing and sales lead generation? Would that be a big part of getting to $2-Million? Yes, of course, and I will share what others are doing in that area. But I will not tell you to go out and spend a bundle on "online" advertising like the consultants do on Facebook.

You probably have enough past customers and potential referrals to bump sales right now without spending much money. I hope you start bidding on bigger jobs shortly, and those do not come from Facebook.

3. YOUR TEAM: Here is the straight-up skinny. You cannot get wealthy on your own. However, you can make $75,000 to $150,000 income as a one or two-person band, but that is it. And God forbid you ever get sick – because your income goes straight to zero that day.

I have a friend in Montana, "Barry," who works in remodeling, he is the typical one-person operation. He is skilled and has done work for Barbara Streisand, Kurt Russell, and many other celebrities over the years.

I tried to get him to hire a crew for a long time, so he would not need to swing a hammer all day. But for some reason, he did not want to take the risk. Well, this past summer, he fell and broke his leg. Broken bones do not heal fast at fifty-nine, and he lost out on the summer building season. Since it is too hard to build in Montana in the winter, he went almost a year without income.

Barry finally started looking for a foreperson who could run a crew of skilled remodelers. Barry has a great personality, and he is a good salesman. Now that Barry understands that younger men should do some jobs, I hope he quickly gets that crew on board. He would not have any problems finding enough work to keep everyone busy. I guess it took falling off a building to force him to do the right thing.

If he decides his first year of having employees went well, I will encourage him to bring on even more people. Barry can sell the jobs, but he will need a couple of forepersons and crackerjack tradespeople to keep up with him. And he will start using my CFO services a lot more to take care of his back office, which he hates doing anyway.

To work around his broken leg, he needs the entire ship's complement. Then if he can not work again sometime in the future, his income will not go to zero for the year.

The nice thing is all these employees will bring in more net income because we were methodical about the growth.

Finding Employees Is a Big Task

For the first few years on your path to $2-million, you need to become a master recruiter. There are skilled and honorable workers out there, but they need a reason to join your team and support your vision. You need to ask them, or they will not come over. In today's market, the most significant shortage is skilled labor (that and lumber). The contractor that has mastered hiring can take on higher-paying projects.

Until you reach $2-million and hire an HR manager, you should figure 20% of your day will be involved in recruiting people. I know that is a lot, but we both know the only reason you are not taking more jobs right now is you cannot get enough people to work.

A part-time CFO can help you craft a benefits package and compensation plan that will keep you cash positive when you bring on more payroll. Forecasting cash flow is what a CFO does best.

On a personal level, I pushed against hiring a lot of employees at first. It scared me because I was not sure I could make payroll or even manage people.

I used one of my vendors as the prime example of being a "rugged individual." This guy lives in Tucson and does telemarketing – you may have even talked to him after you got this book. I knew he was doing $4 million a year, but I thought he was running the entire business out of the barn on his small ranch.

(By the way, he works in his barn because he smokes cigars while on the phone. His wife told him, "you smell like the back end of a horse; go sit out there with the rest of them.)

When I asked him about his team, I thought I would hear about one or two part-time people working from home. I was surprised to hear he had fifty-two employees ranging from salespeople on the phone to an IT department head. He also had a full-time CFO and a half-dozen sales managers, and I had no idea. From Atlanta, the whole operation looks like a one-person band. He told me, 'you don't get to the top by yourself.'

Here is something else I learned: He spends 20% of his week recruiting employees and 30% of his day talking to his existing customers. I was always curious why he had time to help me in my accounting practice and took my calls whenever I had questions.

He told me: "If a customer is not happy enough to recommend me to their mother, I have failed that customer. I talk to my customers because it's the fastest way to get repeat orders and referrals."

He has a scoring system called NPS for "Net Promoter Score." It tells him how likely the customer is to recommend him to others.

The NPS process is why 90% of his revenue is repeat billing from last month. You will find out more about it later in this book. I adopted it myself, and I told all my contractor clients about it.

Most people who build – build again. The highest cost in business development is finding a good, new customer, and once you have one, they can become your repeat and referral revenue for years.

KEY IDEAS:

- Every business owner feels overwhelmed with people who cause chaos. Your life will calm down if you systematically start removing these people from your customer and vendor list.

- Strive to hit $2,000,000 in annual sales; at that level, you can afford to hire better people who will fill in the areas where you are weak.

- The most successful business owners realize that everyone who pays them or receives pay is a human being and being a good 'human engineer' will make your life easier.

- Getting to two million is not impossible. The need for quality contractors is higher in the Atlanta market than at any time in our history.

- Be prepared to dedicate a large chunk of your time to finding and recruiting your team. The good employees are already working, so you must give them a reason to work for you.

CHAPTER 3:
IF I AM SO GOOD, WHY AM I AM NOT ALREADY RICH?

"Jack" was stuck. I had been doing his taxes from the beginning, and he was frustrated.

Four years into running his own construction business, Jack realized he did not have four years of experience; he had one year of experience repeated four times in a row. Nothing had gotten easier.

He was still robbing Peter to pay Paul, did not have enough money in the bank to get that tricked-out F-350 he wanted. He was also working 50 and 60 hours a week to keep the customers from throwing a fit.

On top of that, things at home were not going like Jack promised when he left his $100,000 foreman's job to strike out on his own.

His wife still had to work her day job, and she was up until midnight three times a week doing Jack's bookkeeping. You can bet she was in no mood to hear anything Jack wanted to talk about when she finally did get to bed.

Jack was stuck.

When he left his old job, he thought his boss had it easy, driving a new truck, pulling a 32-foot cruiser out to Lake on the weekend. Heck, the guy even had a small cabin on the water.

Jack had been there a few times on company fishing trips with the other foremen and managers. More than once, Jack sat out on the docks and thought to himself, "If I went out on my own, I could have a place on the water someday."

When Jack brought the idea of starting his own firm home to his wife, she had some dreams too. For the last couple of years, she had wanted to send their two kids to a private Christian school, but the $15,000 a year tuition was so out of their range that she had little hope.

All in all, this "be your own boss" gig was not panning out the way Jack thought it would.

I did Jack's taxes, and he was by no means a failure. Between his draws and his wife's salary, their income was double the average household for   Atlanta, about $140,000 a year. Not bad, but he did put in an incredible number of hours, and all the stress kept him up at night.

What Jack did not know was that I learned more about his past than he expected.

The Thirty-Year Overnight Success

Jack's old boss, Samuel, was not a client of mine. But I met him at a construction trade show once, and we talked for about an hour over coffee. I wanted him to become my client, and he politely explained that he did not need me.

Sam told me he had already implemented the steps I put in place for growing contractors over the past six years. He had a great production team, and his customers loved the work he did so much that the office filled up with cookies every Christmas. Almost all the jobs they take on are repeat sales or referrals.

He was still the head salesman and was so confident in his team that he bid on bigger deals. He even hired a CFO at a $175,000 a year salary, and she was doing a great job making him rich. (A part-time CFO is far cheaper.)

They did not need me. But I did not want to waste an opportunity to learn how he did it.

So, I asked him about going from a three-person show to almost $10-million over six years. His story is a textbook case of "I struggled for years, and I was about to give up, then I discovered___, and now I have success."

What Sam told me was a story of systematically planning to build the employee roster and workflow processes. Sam also motivated his managers to run the business the way he would.

The story started with Sam telling me about the luckiest day of his life. It seems an old-timer looked at him one day back in 2013 and said, "_If you keep doing everything – you're never going to amount to anything."_

At that point, Sam already knew he was slowing down. Revenue was level in the $400,000 a year range, year after year. He was getting bored and maybe a little crazy because he had to do tasks he did not like doing anymore.

Sam was a salesman at heart and hated the accounting part of his business. Worse yet, at fifty years old, he knew his days of swinging a hammer were ending. It had come to where he needed four aspirin before bed to sleep through the back pain. Sam had to do something.

He said to me: "The old-timer's advice, 'you're never going to amount to anything,' kept ringing in my ears."

So, Sam started reading about more prominent contractors. Somewhere along the way, he figured out that every business has three functions, and he could not do all three. Even Elon Musk could not run all three.

Sam shared that when he got to $400,000 in revenue, he was running himself ragged and living on a cash flow roller coaster.

That was until he decided to become a big boy, pull up his J toe boots, and finally get some help.

It only took him thirty years, but Sam learned he could break his business down into three functions:

1. Marketing
2. Production
3. Finance

When you are starting, you must do all three jobs. But if he was going to stop doing everything, he needed to start somewhere.

So, Sam divided the operations into three parts and started building a team of people smarter than he was. One man could run a $400,000 construction business until you got too old or sick to swing a hammer.

But if you ever want to get to $2-million or more, you need to start delegating some of the decisions and responsibilities. To be honest, $400,000 is not a real business; it is a mediocre job without benefits but long hard hours.

Moving From "Hammer Swinging" to Being an Owner

Sam gave up some of the daily micromanaging control he had in the parts of the business that made him tired.

His first hire was a competent foreman (Jack was the third foreman hired, so this is not about him). Hiring in the $100,000 range for a good foreperson was frightening for Sam; he had never left a job site and had no idea what the crew would do if he were not riding herd all day. Even worse, with the firm at $400,000 in revenue, that new foreman would suck up every dime of profit.

Luckily, Sam was an avid reader on how to run a construction business, and he learned that for every $2 in liquid assets or credit lines on the balance sheet, he could spend $1 to hire someone if the move would bring in more money than the new payroll.

That was new information because he had never heard of a formula that would tell you if it was financially smart to hire a manager.

Sam had $100,000 in liquid assets because his wife was frugal, and she remembered every downturn that had happened over the past thirty years. Plus, he had a HELOC with a big enough line that he could cover the rest of the payroll if he needed it. Samuel knew a good man that he had been watching for a few years. The guy was brilliant, but his current boss underpaid him. So, when Sam made the offer, the guy jumped, and Samuel did not know if he should be excited or scared.

Sam told his new foreman: "I am going to put you in charge of getting the jobs done on time and bid. I am giving you the authority and the responsibility to make this next job a winner for the customer and the company. I will bonus out something if you pull it off, but I don't have that figured out yet."

Sam said he would be at the job site every morning to see how they were doing. But once he felt they had a handle on the day, he would leave to bid on more jobs.

Sam knew that if he could spend half his day bidding out work, he would bring in far more money than the $100,000 of new payroll, so he made the hire, and it changed everything.

The second part of the formula looks like this:

If you are going to pay someone $1, they need to bring in $3 minimum. Sam knew he would need to generate $300,000 in additional contracts this year to make the foreman hire work financially.

As soon as Sam started calling on old customers and talking to their neighbors, and following up on bid request sheets, the sales jumped from an average of $35,000 to $50,000 a month.

Then he got hit with a new problem out of the blue.

A vendor called and told Sam he was going on COD until they caught up with the old invoices. Sam did not even know he was delinquent. It became clear that he would need a bookkeeper as well, but he had already stretched his resources to justify the foreman.

Since a bookkeeper at $15 an hour would end up costing $50,000 a year with overhead allocation, Sam knew he would need to pump up the revenue by $450,000 a year instead of only $300,000. But he had never missed a payment in his life and was sick about it.

Sam had been around a long time and knew that he could sell his way out of the business. He had seen more than one guy grow so fast; they went broke.

On top of not getting his bills paid, Sam was worried about job costing and overhead, so he hired a full-time bookkeeper and made her see their accountant twice a month to go over any questions she had about coding transactions.

He knew that paying the accountant $250 an hour, twice a month, would keep problems or confusion from getting to his desk and dragging him away from sales. *Sam knew he needed to be in the market bidding* jobs, not talking to the bookkeeper. So right from the start, he refused to manage the bookkeeper and gave the entire job to his accountant.

He laid the expectations out early with the new bookkeeper:

"Pay the bills on time unless we don't have money, then be smart about how to finagle the invoices a little. Plus, I want to see profit-and-loss statements by the job." (He had to have the P&L by the job because he planned on giving it to the foreman, with the idea that the foreman would make sure they turned a profit or no bonus.)

Now the accountant who had worked for Sam for decades was not too excited about managing the bookkeeper. He was more interested in doing tax returns in the winter and golfing during the summer months. But Sam did a little human engineering on him and convinced him to help him out this year and get the bookkeeper up to snuff.

How to Make Your Accounting a Profit Center

Sam also made another wise observation. Sam knew it would not be long before they hit $85,000 a month in revenue, and if the bookkeeper caught missing change orders, or over inventory that went to the back lot, or kept a careful watch on bad expense tickets, she could save the company 5% of gross, in leakage. Stopping $50,000 a year in leakage was like getting the bookkeeping for free.

Cut your leakage? I asked, Oh sure, every contractor forgets to:

- Bill change orders
- Let's small costs get out of control
- Allows the employees to buy gas for their car on the company's credit card.

As Sam told me: "The bookkeeper's job was to make sure we paid our bills and coded our transactions to the right jobs. And she never let a nickel slip between her fingers on change orders or over-reimbursement to the workers.

"The funny thing was each of these managers I was hiring paid for themselves with increased billing or slashing costs. But I had to watch it like a hawk; I poured over those profit-and-loss statements every week, and it almost drove our accountant crazy with all our questions."

Well, within the year, the revenue had jumped to $85,000 a month - about $1 million a year because Sam could finally put in four hours a day drumming up contracts. At that point, he decided he could set up two more crews over the next year, and so he hired two more forepersons, including our boy, Jack.

Sam felt like a new man. He spent his time building relationships and bidding jobs, and the open ones on the board grew every week. Even better, they were coming in close to being on time, and he thought on a budget, but was not sure about that end of it.

I sat amazed at Sam's story, so I wanted to sum it up.

I said, "At $400,000 a year, or an average of $35,000 a month, you hired a foreman that allowed you to become a dedicated salesman. That worked, and orders started rolling in.

"At $50,000 a month, you got a full-time bookkeeper but felt you should have done it a year earlier once you realized how much chaos the financial end of the business was causing. And worrying about money was the biggest reason you could not sleep at night.

"Then you were free from running the crew and handling the books, and you had enough time to double sales again over the next year. That gave you the confidence to bring on two more forepersons and give them the okay to build their crew of employees and subcontractors.

"I believe you told the new guys: 'Bring the jobs in on time and budget and make sure that when I go out to see the customer, they are delighted with our work. Pull that off, and we are golden.'"

That is how in 12 months, Sam moved from a $400,000 a year business to $1-million a year. Furthermore, it looked like he could double the billing to $2-million the following year. The sales turned out to be easy because he was in the field bidding jobs.

The foremen were doing their jobs, and the bookkeeper was checking all the boxes, but he was still nervous about the net profit. The place was out of control regarding money management and delivering raw materials on time to the job sites. The company was breaking even, but Sam felt he should drop 20% to the bottom line.

Sam went on to tell me how important the profit margins were because he saw a lot of bigger jobs on the horizon. Jobs they could not bid on Jobs because he would need access to some hefty lines of credit to pull it off. If he went to the bank with financials that did not show a profit, they would laugh him out the back door. So he was still turning down deals.

The bookkeeper did not have the gravitas to handle such a thing, and Sam's accountant was playing golf. The one missing function in his business was a numbers man. The bookkeeper was not up to being a CFO.

Sam also needed someone who could work with the banks and line up more production credit. His employees were complaining about the benefits package, and he needed it updated. Some of his jobs were behind because no one made sure the raw materials were delivered when required.

Sam told me he wanted to bid on bigger jobs, but his back office problems kept sucking him back to his desk, doing work he did not like to do.

The bookkeeper was good in her limited role. But she spent most of her time worrying about getting the bills and payroll done on time and did not know how to set up financial and workflow management systems.

At this point, Sam was asking more of his bookkeeper than she could deliver, and they were both frustrated. She almost lived at the accountant's office trying to keep up, and the $250 an hour was costing Sam around $2,000 a month now. Managing the bookkeeper was now costing almost as much as the bookkeeper herself.

> **HUMAN ENGINEERING TIP:** If an employee does not do what you tell them, it is almost always because they do not know how to do it.

His accountant had about enough of him, too, by telling him, "My job is not to run your business. I do tax returns and help people with their QuickBooks. If you have a tax problem, I will fix it. If you think you are overpaying taxes, I will figure it out. But running your business is beyond what I will do."

Sam knew then he had the wrong money man in place. He needed to stop growing at around $100,000 a month because cash flow was awful, and his reserve accounts were almost down to zero. Maybe he was selling his way out of business.

At this point, Sam realized he had to fill out that circle and bring in a CFO if he was going to achieve $2-million and beyond.

A Game-Changing Hire

Sam did not know back then that you could hire a CFO part-time, someone like me with construction knowledge, but does not require $175,000 a year plus benefits to solve the problems.

So, he gritted his teeth and pulled the trigger. He told me he found a sharp young woman whose father had owned a significant construction company in Dallas. She wanted to prove herself and go out on her own. Sam told me he was shocked by the salary requirement. He knew a good CPA was only about $75,000 a year and a crackerjack was less than $125,000. How could he ever justify paying this college girl such big money?

Then she did something that Sam never expected. She told him she had to go over his accounting records before she would accept the job.

She spent three days in the office going over the profit-and-loss statements and the balance sheet line by line. But it did not stop there. She reviewed the open jobs board, talked to some of their past customers, and even went to see two of his local vendors. Then she stopped by the job site and took the foreman to lunch to find out what he thought Sam could do better to help the foreman.

Sam had never seen anything like it. No employee had ever sat down and said, "I will not take the job unless I can impact the business." This young woman invested a week in his business before she received one dime.

When she came back in with her report, she laid out a case study for taking Sam to $10-million in revenue. She said it would take four to six years, and we would need to borrow money from the bank to finance the negative cash flow that she was sure was on the horizon.

Sam looked at the report, then looked at the young woman. He realized he had never met anyone who understood the opportunities and dangers like this college girl in thirty-five years of running a business.

He smiled at her and said, "I have no idea how I will swing your paycheck, and I may need to pay you with my wife's Visa card for the first few months. If you think we can do this, I think we can do this. I know there are bigger jobs out there, but I believe we can pull it off with the foreman, my sales skills, and someone running this office. You are hired."

Now I was sitting there with Sam for almost an hour, and my coffee was cold. But I was fascinated with the story. It was so rare to find someone who looked at every situation and said, "Yes, and then we can do this bigger thing next."

Before trying anything new, most business owners tell you what won't work and how many conditions they need. Sam was different; he was ready to make it happen and solve the problems holding him back as he went along.

I had to summarize everything that Sam had told me over the past 60 minutes.

"So, Sam, help me understand...you were in business for decades, and your revenue was stuck at $35,000 a month. Then you hear from an old-timer that says you will never amount to anything if you do not hire somebody to help, and you decide to take the advice.

"You began by bringing in production people (foremen) to get the work done, which freed you up to be the salesperson. That was important because, like all businesses, the company has three functions: marketing, finance, and production."

"You decided you were better at marketing than anything else because you were tired of swinging a hammer and walking through muddy job sites. So, you started bringing in foremen, even to the point that you let them hire their own crews and take responsibility for bringing the jobs in on time and budget."

But that was not the entire story, so I went on:

"You were afraid that at $1 million in annual revenue, the money might be out of control, and there was a possibility you were going to sell your way into bankruptcy. So, you made the riskiest choice of all and hired a young college girl to become the finance manager."

"She stepped in and did what I do for my clients: lined out the type of work you should do, focused on job costing and profit margins, *and* made sure you had the credit available to carry over the negative cash flow periods as you grew the business."

"So, here you are seven years after the day the guy told you to pull up your cowboy boots and get some help, and you are closing in on $10-million in revenue right on schedule."

"Sam, this was the most impactful one hour I have spent since the day I got married. Thank you."

I meant every word. We are still friends, and I love catching up with him at trade shows and association meetings.

CHAPTER 4:
JACK'S JOURNEY TO
$2-MILLION

Now back to Jack...

When we first met, he was just starting out and only wanted an accountant to do his taxes and payroll. I agreed because I felt Jack had the determination to make it happen. We take on lots of smaller firms where we see the right attitude.

It was not until Jack came in complaining about being in business for four years and nothing happening that I told him I had met his old boss. I assured him that Sam had no animosity towards Jack for leaving and starting his own company. I heard that he even sent a few of the smaller jobs that did not fit their business model to help Jack get started.

When I told Jack the story that I recounted in the last chapter, he looked at me and said, "Well, Sam taught me everything I know about running a crew, but he did not teach me everything he knows about running a business. I guess I need help."

Jack was wondering why it was so hard to get to where he could have a cabin out on Lake Lanier, too. Maybe even a boat tied up to the dock. His next question was whether he should first hire a foreman, a salesman, or a money man and whether he could afford any of them.

Well, the first step in getting Jack to $2-million was simple. He had to determine for himself what he liked to do.

So, I asked him: Do you enjoy bidding for the jobs? Do you enjoy doing the work? Or are you drawn to the back office working on the spreadsheets and project management Gantt charts and making sure the bookkeeper is doing the right job?

I did not see any reason to make a big deal out of it because every single contractor I have known over the last twenty years has said they want to bid on the work or do the jobs. No one wants to be the money man.

Some contractors are a little afraid of letting someone else manage the money, but that is an unfounded fear. The real danger is not knowing the numbers and making business decisions based on gut feelings. The real cost is losing opportunities to grow because you do not have the gravitas to pull off the bigger jobs.

Jack was thirty years old, strong, and loved being outside, and took great personal satisfaction in seeing his projects through to completion. Nothing made him happier than a customer gushing all over a new deck or bathroom or kitchen. Okay, we settled it; I told him; you are the production manager. Now we had to figure out how to manage the money and the sales.

Can You Handle the Truth?

Now, I was reluctant to tell Jack the next truth. But he had to know it.

So, I told him, "At your level of business, with the amount of money you have in reserve, you are not strong enough to hire a manager in any of these three functions."

Then I had to give him even more bad news: "You are spending too much of the company's cash. I strongly recommend that you figure out how much money you need to live on and make that your salary. The two of you make around $12,000 a month–I believe you should cut that back to $10,000. But it would be better if you could do $8,000. That gives you a budget to hire, and Jack, you need help."

"We can bump you back up to $12,000 in a year if you are finally getting this show on the road. If you have dreams of buying a cabin and a boat before you have this company at $2-million in revenue, I do not want to work with you."

I explained that people who treat their business account as a personal piggy bank never get ahead. I added it would be a waste of time and energy to start working to $2-million if you did not stop co-mingling personal and business money, and you must get financial controls in place.

"You better fall in love with your old truck and your track house because that is as good as it gets until you hit the $2-million mark. Can you live with that?"

Jack was a little hesitant about that; he wanted a boat.

I explained that if he showed some financial discipline and a willingness to work smarter than 98% of the people in America, in five years, he could live the rest of his life like most people only dreamed about.

I would show him how. I would help him run the money. But it would be up to Jack if it happens or not. "Besides," I told him, "Your old boss would probably take you out on his boat anytime you want if you fill it up with gas. Believe me, $400 in his gas tank will be cheaper than owning a boat."

I told Jack from that day forward every dime he made over his monthly salary (and, yes, he was going on payroll with taxes deducted like a proper business) was going to be pulled out of the business and put into an outside investment fund.

That cash would work on its own in the background. Eventually, this investment income would exceed business income. By the way, that is the point when you feel rich. The day your investments make more than your day job.

Plus, we would need that investment fund as collateral to borrow at the bank as the business grows. There may come a day when the bank likes you so much, they would not require additional collateral, I explained, but today is not that day.

Then Jack asked, "Why not leave the cash in the business, so we do not need to borrow? Would we not have ready funds to keep moving forward?"

No, when you have a hoard of cash on hand, you make poor decisions.

I told him about another contractor who had built up an $80,000 reserve and held it in his business checking account. Then, every time a marketing salesperson called, he would say to himself, "$850 is not so bad; I have $80,000, and I can afford that."

The same thing happened when he saw lumber on sale or a good deal on a new piece of equipment. And bam, the money was gone, forever.

"If you want to get to $2-million and drop 20% to the bottom line, we need to learn how to run lean and mean all the time," I said to Jack. "I want you to think you are always broke and must get the next job done, or you cannot make payroll. As the old Rocky song goes, I need to see some 'eye of the tiger' from you."

That was a lot of truth to dump on Jack, but I wanted to see if he was a "yes, and _____" type of guy.

HUMAN ENGINEERING TIP: There are three types of businesspeople in the world.

Some will listen to an idea or proposal and say "Yes, but _____." They always have a reason something will not work. These people will only get by with the bare minimum. They are terrible customers because you get pushed back at every level of the job.

The second type of person will answer a proposal with "Yes, if _____." The yes if, guy has a lot of conditions, and he wants to push the responsibility of his success onto your shoulders. You can work with the "Yes, if" people. But they are going to be hard to make happy.

The best type of customer is the one who says, "Yes, and if we do that, then we can do this."

When you find people who are forward-thinking like that, do everything you can to get close. If you have twenty-five "Yes, and" people in your life, you are going to accomplish everything you ever dreamed about. The hard part is that it can take years to find twenty-five, but it is worth the work.

In my own practice, even if we start small, I bend over backward to get the "yes, and" businessperson as a client. They are going places, and I want to be along for the ride.

When I interview potential business clients, I am on the lookout for how they respond to my suggestions. In Jack's case, he said, "Yes, and if we can get even close to what Sam is doing in his business, I can do _____." That was what I was hoping to hear.

I tell my contractors to use the "Yes, and," "Yes, if," and "Yes, but" responses to determine the character of the person they are dealing. If they plan on dumping the eventual outcome back on your shoulders and probably sabotage the project along the way, you need to be aware of that upfront. (And of course, the exception is if everything goes right, they will take the credit. But so what, you got the money.)

FOOTNOTE: I even listen for the "yes, but" when deciding if I can give an employee more responsibility.

Jack agreed to live within his means, so I gave him the next steps:

4. You are going to have to run your crew and make the sales. For now, you get both jobs because you cannot afford to bring on a managing foreman or a rock star salesman at this time.

5. I would do your bookkeeping and act as your CFO. I would be the money man you need. I could start impacting your business immediately because I don't need any ramp-up time to understand your business. Plus, I have done this before.

6. I would help you figure out what type of work you do best and work with the bank to get more funding and a host of other services you need. I would do this job until you get to $10-million. Then you need to fire me and hire an in-house full-time CFO.

Then Jack shared how he was worried about the cost of this plan.

So, I said to him, "Jack, I know about your financial situation. The truth is, you could not afford it if I charged you minimum wage. But if you doubled your gross sales this year, then no matter what you pay me, I would be the best bargain you have ever enjoyed."

"My current contractors have a choice of good-better-best service that ranges from $12,000 a year to $100,000.

"Don't forget to breathe, Jack; I know you can't pay me $100,000.

"We will start small and see how we do as we go along. But Jack, if I can hold your hand this year and move you from $300,000 in billing to $600,000, you will find that a management team will generate more revenue than they cost and be whistling Dixie to the bank.

"It is like buying a dirt lot for $1 million. You do not care about the price if you can build a house on it for $750,000 and sell that house for $2.5 million next year."

Now, let's look at what a part-time CFO does and why hiring one is an investment with a fast ROI.

CHAPTER 5:
ARE YOU WASTING YOUR DAY WORKING ON THE WRONG THINGS?

I n Chapter 3, I introduced you to Sam and how he discovered the three functions in any business: sales, finance, and production.

Sam found people smarter than he was and gave them the authority to do their section of the business. He discovered good people bring in more money than they cost in payroll, so it was a good business move. As a result, Sam is on his way to $10-million.

In this chapter, you will understand two more critical decisions you must make to get to $2-million

1. Without good financial controls and usable numbers, you should stay right where you are. Do not grow anymore, or you may grow out of business. Growth feeds chaos, and you must kill the chaos first, or it will lead to bankruptcy or heart attack.

   That means you must track everything. Set up reporting on every step you take toward $2-million. If you run an ad, you must know how many calls came in, how many of those leads converted to sales, and whether those sales were profitable. Buying advertising is the easiest example to understand. But everything in your business should have systems in place that allow you to track and measure results. It is vital to set up the tracking systems now before you end up committing the 'sin-of-the-inaccurate-assumption.'

Without good numbers, you will guess. Guessing is chaos that leads to mistakes. Mistakes that can go on until you are broke. As humans, we tend to adopt the fallacy-of-the-sunken-cost. That means we have so much wrapped up in a mistake that we are afraid to fix the error. Remember the number one reason business owners give when asked why they failed at something is 'I waited too long to _____.' You can fill in the blank.

2. Everyone has one good thing they do better than anybody else, and we do that one thing for one type of customer. By digging into your past results hidden in your accounting software, we will find your 'good build' and focus all your energy toward getting it done often and at high-profit margins.

Introducing The 80/20 Rule

In every business, 20% of the people you work for generate 80% of your profit.

I will repeat that about a dozen more times in the following 50 pages–it's critical information.

What that means to you is that in a typical 50-hour workweek, about 12 hours were profitable, and 38 hours were "activity." You did a lot of work with little and sometimes negative impact on your bottom line, and I will prove that in this chapter.

The 80/20 rule runs through every part of our lives.

- You have some employees who look busy all the time, but you may discover they are not making you any profit. To them, the definition of work is activity, not an accomplishment, and it costs you a bundle.

- You probably have vendors who act like they are bending over backward for you. After careful review, you find out that you can get easier terms, better pricing, and dependable delivery elsewhere.

- But the most common 80/20 offender could be one of your biggest customers. The guy who sends you a lot of work but always asks for discounts and then never stops pushing you to absorb the cost of minor changes or delays in paying you or a hundred other minor friction points. You end up spending hundreds of unplanned hours keeping your "best" customer happy. It may turn out that your biggest customer is doing more to put you in the poorhouse than your ex.

However, I guess you do not believe me, or you're convinced that your intuition has the problems under control.

So, in this chapter, we will analyze your past jobs, so it will become painfully evident that you are not exempt from the 80/20 rule. You have probably spent 80% of your energy on projects that you could have skipped and ended up with the same take-home pay in the past year.

Our task is to determine why 20% of your customers were profitable and repeat what you did for those customers. Then you repeat the wins so often that you do not have time for the dangerous projects. At the end of the year, you are more profitable.

Now, I know you dislike thinking about bookkeeping, and it looks like an enormous waste of time and money because all we want is to get the payroll out on time and keep our vendors paid. We also do not want to go to jail for bad tax returns.

As far as most contractors can see, nothing I've just told you is worth the cost of getting accurate numbers and usable reports from your accounting software. But if your books are off or you don't take the time to go over the reports, you are guessing which jobs, people, vendors, and services are making money. Guessing never works.

You already have answers to the question "How do I get rich?" hidden in your accounting. We just need to put it into black and white, so you are forced to manage by the numbers.

Accountants only worry about balance sheets and tax returns, and marketing people want to generate leads and bring in more jobs. Only a CFO understands that the secret to getting rich is already there, waiting for you to uncover it.

Now, that is important. When most contractors decide they want to build revenue, the first thing they do is buy advertising, which is nuts. You have no idea who will see your advertising, which means you cannot control the type of customer you will deal with or what they expect you to deliver. Advertising attracts unreasonable customers. Referrals and repeat business are a better path to wealth.

In your journey to $2-million, you cannot start buying advertising or throwing bids at every job that comes, or you will put yourself out of business by growing too fast or doing the wrong jobs.

Growth without focus and controls in place is dangerous. You have seen enough flash-in-the-pan hot-shots to know this is true.

But with good bookkeeping, a CFO can start analyzing your business and putting it on a path for sustainable, steady, and safe growth.

A CFO can determine:

- What type of work are you good at?
- What kind of customer do you like?
- What part of town should you be focusing on?
- Which employee or team drives the most profit.
- Whether you have your job costing, change orders, and bidding under control.
- If you are making money on every job and why.

Now that last one is important. If you made a great profit on your previous job, you must understand what went right so you can tell your crew and make sure they repeat the process.

HUMAN ENGINEERING TIP: In managing, most of our effort focuses on who made an error. Trying to fix humans is difficult. It is better to figure out why something went wrong and fix that instead. You can engineer most problems out of your life before they happen.

These are more management numbers a part-time CFO will bring to the table. We will go over those in the marketing section of this book.

Wisdom Versus Knowledge

Here is knowledge: The path to $2-million hides in plain sight, inside your accounting.

Here is wisdom: Understanding the accounting and acting on it with a deadline for each step.

The most successful contractors I know have figured out how to use past results to help them focus on future opportunities. They know what they did last year that worked well and focus on a limited number of opportunities that match their 20% profile. Using knowledge to make good decisions is the definition of wisdom.

You will end up doing a lot of that "one thing," so it becomes second nature for the office team and field crew. You get a reputation for being so good at that "one thing" they cannot ignore you. Everyone on the team knows what to do in almost every situation because the work is second nature. That means less training, cost overruns, and customer complaints.

Here are two more examples that I picked out from my clients that show this in action.

"Mike" had an opportunity to build a 5,000-square-foot custom home. However, the customer wanted to use a new process for pouring concrete walls, prefab blocks, and built-in solar tiles on the roof.

Mike had no idea how it worked. But he wanted the deal because it might be a foothold in a market he wanted to try.. When they went over the blueprints, the foreman thought about the job and said, "Mike, since our crew knows nothing about this new technology, our productivity is going to suck. We may not turn a profit on this job. On top of that, you will need to stop making sales calls for the next two months because this will bring big questions to the job site. You need to be there almost all the time."

Mike had enough wisdom to understand that no sales calls for two months would mean employee layoffs in five months. It was a great opportunity, but Mike understood his limitations, so he passed on the bid.

Another client, "Master" (what a great first name, eh?), decided that buying older homes going through gentrification to bring them up to modern standards would be a great opportunity. He could turn a few mansions a year and maybe net $100,000 or more on each of them. So, Master bought his first "flip," as they call it, on a late-night infomercial.

What Master found out was that his crew was great at putting up million-dollar homes on a flat slab, but in an old mansion, everything was a "one-off," as the British love to say. There was no standardization in anything they did; it was almost like creating art every day on the job.

Of course, you know where this ended, and Master was lucky to get out without losing his pants. The $100,000 dream faded quickly.

KEY IDEA:

Every contractor who has been swinging a hammer for two years has developed an instinct for certain types of work. If you figure out what that is by carefully analyzing your past jobs, you can plan for your crew to do a lot more of that "one thing."

Your best jobs from the last two years will become the model for your minimum contract from now on.

CHAPTER 6:
ARE YOU READING FINANCIAL STATEMENTS LIKE A TOM CLANCY NOVEL?

When I go into a business doing under $2-million in revenue, the owner is usually working on some type of advertising plan to bring in the next job.

When I go to larger companies, the owner is pouring over their last job's financial reports to analyze what they did right or what went wrong. They look at spreadsheets like a page-turner spy novel.

Maybe those big dogs know something you don't, and you can bet they did not wait until they hit $2-million to use their numbers to manage the business. They started the first time they felt like their construction business had become nothing more than 50 or 60 hours a week of hard labor, missed school plays, and worrying about covering payroll.

Your success is not a mystery. A CFO that knows construction will find the clues that uncover the truth.

Almost every successful contractor gets someone to help make sense of their costs and figure out where they should look for bigger contracts and what financing they can get, making the operation less stressful. They know their future success is somewhere on a spreadsheet.

That is management accounting; it is above and beyond what a bookkeeper or a tax preparer offers.

Sometimes understanding our numbers leads us to the perfect business–the one we already have.

While "Robert" stood in the small bathroom and listened as the homeowner went on about the "lavender" she picked out for the walls, he thought to himself it was $3,000 for fixtures and supplies and $3,000 more to stand here and listen to wall color talk.

Why did I get into this business, he wondered?

As the years went on, Robert was not getting rich. He was still working 12-hour days, and he knew he was getting too old to crawl under sinks someday. He had to figure something out.

One of Robert's problems was that he could not see past Friday when he needed enough cash in the bank to draw out rent and grocery money even after years in the business. Good thinking if they limit it to the short term, but it is a terrible strategy if you want to create a company you are proud of and make life for your family more comfortable.

Robert was running his bathroom remodeling business on what we call COH accounting. Every morning, he would look online to see if he had enough cash-on-hand (COH) to cover today's needs. Robert had pushed back on tax planning, saying it was too expensive. And he was happy with the $15 an hour bookkeeper he had because she did the payroll on time, and no checks had bounced for over a year.

The bookkeeper was a pleasant woman, but she was incompetent at creating usable reports built around KPI numbers (key performance indicators). It was so bad that Robert did not even read his profit-and-loss statement because he knew it was inaccurate.

Unfortunately, he was fearful of getting out of bathroom remodels since he did not know how his business was doing. At $15 an hour, the bookkeeper costs Robert around $60,000 a year when you include the benefits and overhead allocation. So, for $60,000, Robert got his bills paid and payroll, which was not much for that amount of money.

Robert was probably going nowhere but the plumbing department at the Home Depot for the rest of his life. But he knew he hated bathrooms and wanted to do something about it.

Robert had another problem: cash flow. Since he had resorted to COH accounting, he did not know why he was always out of money. He was optimistic that his cash flow problems would disappear if he started building luxury homes or apartment buildings. That was an inaccurate assumption.

Robert did not know it, but without useful financial reports, any strategy he came up with to improve the business was wishful thinking. The problems he had today were still going to be with him next year, but they would be a lot bigger if he left bathroom remodels. He knew everything about bathrooms; he knew little about million-dollar homes.

As my favorite philosopher, Dirty Harry, once said, "A man has to know his limitations."

The Turning Point

What Robert needed was an objective voice of reason that could point out where the business stood at the end of the day so he could adjust what he charged or how fast he collected his retainers.

He was skilled as a contractor but terrible at running an actual business. He wanted to set up crews to do the work, but he did not see how to afford it. So, he stayed small out of fear.

When Robert finally agreed to a mid-year tax planning meeting, he broke out in frustration and talked about his business. I told him he could tighten up the ship and use it to springboard into building luxury homes but that he had to do it one step at a time. But he first needed to analyze what he was doing currently, or it would be too risky to take on bigger projects.

Now that last paragraph causes a lot of uncomfortable feelings for most contractors. We're convinced that our gut instinct should be right. But the sin of the inaccurate assumption has put a lot of guys out of business.

I told Robert it would take a year, maybe two, to get out of the bathroom once and for all. He was in a rut, and those are tough to fix for anyone in business.

I laid out a game plan and gave Robert a "good-better-best" pricing scheme, so he could move forward at a speed that made him comfortable. No accountant wants to be the reason you cannot sleep at night worrying about money.

What I Needed Robert to Discover About His Construction Business

When I started working with him, I gave Robert homework. I asked him to print out a list of his jobs over the past two years. To jot down notes about how much he made from the job, how he found the customer, and what problems he encountered in getting the work done.

I was looking for a pattern on what Robert could do well today and what he could do in the future based on the team he had in place.

Robert did not do his homework. He came back and said, "I do not know how to allocate overhead, and I can only guess our job costs. It seems the bookkeeper lumped most of our bills into one overhead account. So, I don't know if we made a profit. I need you to do this for me if we will never get it done."

I knew he was going to give me the job back. It is tedious work and easy to make big assumptions and errors that lead to incorrect conclusions. Making the mistake of the inaccurate assumption is the second-worst mistake you can make in business. It is almost always fatal. (I know I'm repeating myself here, but this is critical wisdom.)

Oh, and the number one mistake? Well, that's a fill-in-the-blank. When you ask any business owner what went wrong? They always say: "I waited too long to _____." You can fill in the blank, but the answer is always the same: you should have seen that problem long before it bit you in the butt. That is why we all need an advisor looking over our business.

An experienced advisor will point out when you are waiting too long to fix something or, like a character in an Ernest Hemingway novel said when asked how he went bankrupt: "Well, it was slow at first, but pretty quick at the end."

I know you want to grow your business. But here is a fact: you must start where you already are. You cannot close the doors on Friday with the idea that you are a different company on Monday. (Remember that human engineering pertains to the owner too.) you would not know how to be that "new" company, and you would end up right back in the lavender bathroom.

Migrating to a high-dollar, high-profit construction company takes a plan. The plan is simple because you base it on what you are already doing. Even the process for change is fun because every day, you see things getting better. The less chaos in your business, the more often you eat dinner with your kids.

However, a plan on paper means nothing. It is about as good as clicking on the Amazon wish list, hoping someone you know sends you a gift. You must convert plans to calendar dates; specific action steps with a deadline assigned to your team. Then you must move forward one step at a time.

Is it worth the expense and money to change directions? Only you can answer that. But in my experience, five years from now, you will be five years older, whether you are rich or not.

So, you might as well get a plan on the calendar and 'get rich or die trying.' (Thanks, 50 Cent; that is a brilliant line.)

The Discovery Process

The time had come to get to work with Robert.

Step One: I had Robert open his QuickBooks files so we could print out a list of all the jobs he did over the past two years. We needed a lot of information about those jobs:

- How much did you bid the job for initially?
- How much did you end up charging in total?
- Did you bill for those change orders?
- What was your labor cost, including your time as the owner?
- What kind of markup did you get on the supplies and fixtures?
- What was the margin of profit after you finished the job?
- Did you allocate overhead properly to each job over the year?

We were looking at all this through the angle of the 80/20 rule.

Most of the time, the problem is in the 80%. Most of our jobs are break-even (but you would not know unless you have good numbers), or they might cost us more than we get paid. If you do not allocate overhead properly as you go along, it is difficult to pinpoint how many of our jobs are a waste of time.

If we ignored overhead allocation, we could fool ourselves into believing that we were making money, but we did not come close. I swear some jobs I have seen contractors take on are so fraught with danger that I think they would be better off mailing the client a $5,000 check and tell them to take the bid elsewhere. It would be cheaper in the long run.

The good news is that some customers were better for Robert. Some types of work fit his personality and skill set. The bids were fair, and the customer will finance the job as he went.

The goal here is to know all we can about the 20% of our past efforts that worked and duplicate them.

So, to get rich, we find your sweet spot customer, the one buying the high-profit services, and then focus all your efforts on duplicating that project with that kind of customer.

I tell my contractors after we do this exercise to take the profile of the best 20% of their jobs and make that the new floor. Any job that comes in must fit the 20% profile from this day forward or don't bid.

That alone can double your net profits inside a year because you stop the chaos before it gets in the front door. Chaos sucks up your time and your soul. Get rid of it, and you can focus on more of what works. Plus, working without chaos is fun.

But remember, I cannot pull the rug out on bathrooms for Robert on Monday morning, or his kids would not have Cheerios on the breakfast table. Making those financial decisions is why a basic bookkeeper gets so frustrated in most construction companies.

Deciding on what type of work you should bid on and the type of customer you want to work for is why you need the business analysis skills a CFO brings to the table.

Before I completed a job-by-job analysis, I asked Robert to take the list and answer some questions for me about each job. It only took about 20 minutes, and there was a lot he did not remember. But here is what I wanted to know:

1. Did you like the customer?

2. What was the age and sex of the customer?

3. How did you find the job?

4. Did the customer give you any referrals that led to more work?

5. What kind of work did you do?

6. What was the worst thing that happened at that job?

7. Do you feel the job was profitable?

8. If I called that customer today, would they give you a glowing recommendation?

Robert did not remember everything, but we got enough down on paper to figure out what step on the ladder we should use as the minimum client in the future.

Then I had to ask Robert a few more questions that fell under the category of marketing to see if Robert had someone skilled enough to use the data wisely. Until then, I would do it.

- If you painted a picture of your six best builds this past year, what did they look like?

- Who is buying that type of work? Describe that person as if they were sitting across from you.

- What does that buyer look for in a contractor?

- Is there anything you need to improve to be that guy?

- What kind of capital do you need to swing bigger jobs?

There were a lot of unknowns. What you can take away from the second list of questions is that a CFO does a lot more than work numbers–they do human engineering, as well.

HUMAN ENGINEERING TIP: Unknowns cause confusion and fear. All confused people do the same thing; they STOP. If you have a tradesman or a customer that stops on you, it may well be that they are confused. It is your job as the owner to figure that out and take steps to fix it.

Robert's Shocking Realization

We never got past the point of analyzing Robert's current business.

I thought he wanted to move out of lavender bathrooms and start building million-dollar homes. It turned out that he liked his business; he was only tired of the chaos and looking over the fence for greener pastures. After seeing that some of his jobs were rewarding, he asked me how to work on the fun stuff and get the soul-sucking grind off his plate.

So, I asked Robert the most critical question of the day.

Will you make a list of everything you do this week? List every time you answer the phone, write up a bid, or pay a bill; I want a list of everything.

I do not care how many times you do it or how much time it takes; I explained, I want to see a list of all the different tasks that you touch.

Easy worksheet for getting chaos out of your life.

For the next three to five days, keep this paper close. Every time you engage in a task, no matter how simple, write that task down.

You only need to list them one time. So, only put 'answered the phone from a vendor' on the report once. Select if the task is a 'pig' that's something you dislike doing. It might be a 'cash cow' that's a job you are competent at, but it does not interest you anymore. The right column is where you check your 'racehorses'; these are tasks that have you smiling while doing them. In five days, you will clearly understand why you go home exhausted. I'm guessing you spend about 80% of your time on 'pigs,' and it is wearing you out.

LIST EACH TASK ONE TIME	🐖	🐄	🐎

You may download this worksheet in MS WORD by going to our website, go.bottomline.tax/contractors, and click on the menu item 'worksheets.'

What you are trying to figure out is what you should STOP doing.

So, I texted Robert for the next five days to remind him to work on the list. I was beside myself with excitement. The impact on Roberts' life was going to be sweeter than stolen honey. He had no idea how this simple list would make his life about ten times better.

The following week, in our management meeting, I took the list and asked Robert to put a red line through everything he did not like to do. I did not care if it was critical work or if he was the only one competent at it. I did not care if he did not have someone that could take over that one job.

I wanted to know what he no longer enjoyed doing. It took him a half-hour because he felt morally obligated to do work he did not want to do. It seemed to me he was hearing his father's voice from childhood.

I then told him the golden words:

Everything on this list that you do not like doing–STOP DOING IT.

The bottom line was I gave Robert emotional permission to stop doing things he hated. He was doing these tasks poorly anyway, so get rid of it and grow this business to $2-million. Now Robert would have the time to do the right thing.

He responded: 'Yes and ____" and I was jumping for joy because I knew he was going to make it big. Robert stayed in the bathroom.

The conclusions Robert came up with on his own were stellar.

- I don't need to do the pigs and cash cows, and I can engineer the task out of our process or hire someone else to do it.
- I need to bring in help with the production work (a foreman or tradesman) and stop crawling under sinks.

- I need financial and operations management, so I am not up all night worrying about the money.

- I need to stop doing chaotic jobs that do not fit my sweet spot.

Now, all Robert had to do was get rid of what he did not like doing, and everything else would be fun. But that meant he needed to write about how he wanted problems and opportunities handled. They all don't need to be done at once, I assured him. Let's wait until something happens on your pig's list, and we'll fix it then.

I was also happy to share that we had a lot of experience with operations manuals and would be glad to review his progress as he went along.

Robert took on sales and bidding but hopes to hire for that job as well next year. I became his CFO part-time for about one-fifth the cost of hiring someone who knew construction. In short order, we brought in a young foreman who put together a two-person crew.

The new hires, cash flowed out because sales went up dramatically with each new manager on the team. I still had to watch the cash flow like a hawk, so I met with Robert in a Zoom meeting every week for the first two years.

Robert is now one of the top bathroom remodelers in Georgia. He is working less than 40 hours a week, and you have never seen a happier soul. He is fat and sassy today.

TIP: USING YOUR PHONE TO CREATE "HOW WE DO IT HERE:" Before Robert could move the production work off his plate, he needed to create a process for his foreman to follow when finishing a job. Lavender bathrooms were easy for Robert; he had done it hundreds of times.

But no foreman he hired would know as much as Robert, and if he did not want to get sucked back under the sink, he needed to transfer his knowledge. His teenage daughter solved the problem.

She explained to Robert how to use his mobile phone every time the customer asked a question, or Robert made a decision or found an unexpected problem in the wall behind the sink.

She suggested Robert record a short video clip as she did on her YouTube and Tik-Tok channels. She was trying to become an 'influencer' and had developed a lot of skill in being precise and entertaining in her clips.

So, he grabbed his phone and started making a video where he would talk the problem and solution out, showing how he explained it to the customer

Those video clips were awful, but they transferred years of wisdom to the new foreman. It surprised Robert that he could explain a complicated situation by just talking as he videoed the problem in just a few minutes.

His daughter titled and summarized the videos so they could be searched easily. She then created a YouTube channel and uploaded them as dad brought new ones home. Now Robert had a permanent record of how to remodel a bathroom.

There were three advantages:

1. His foreman could use his phone to look up solutions or even post questions to Robert.

2. Potential customers always look you up online nowadays, so those video clips gave him some credibility in the decision process.

3. The video clips got some new customers on the phone because Robert looked so sincere as he explained how we do it here.

So, with the 80/20 question nailed, are you ready to bring on new customers?

Well, not yet.

You have probably had workflow or production consultants who banter a million-dollar jump if you give them $25,000 to write operations manuals for you. You are probably getting calls from online marketing "gurus" who say they will make your phone ring for $2,000 a month base plus a $3,000 ad budget. I recommend caution here.

If you do not tie the extra activity to financials, you will not understand if it is working or not. Remember the number one reason a business fails: "I waited too long to _____." Random advertising is one of the easiest ways to waste money, and guessing is the easiest way to 'wait too long.'

To drive your business to the next level, always start with the customers you have, build detailed money tracking systems and production processes, and find people to manage the three parts of your business.

But here is the kicker:

If you systematically implement the concepts and processes outlined in this book, you may not need to generate a bunch of marginal leads. Your referrals and repeat orders will build your business at a better profit margin than the price shopper a webpage brings in.

The advantage of working with an accountant as your part-time CFO is that we have seen dozens of operations like yours; you are getting a lot of experience, knowledge, and wisdom on your team instantly. We can see when you are going off the rails and bring you back to earth in our weekly meetings.

That is because mistakes show up quickly in your accounting if you have good cost accounting tied to every job, employee, and promotion. We will make sure you do not go another day without doing the right thing.

Now, I realize you may already have someone doing your bookkeeping, and you probably love the CPA who does your tax returns. You may have been with them for years. If you want to keep your CPA but get rid of the chaos, maybe we can streamline your business while acting as your liaison to your tax preparer and provide them with the numbers they need to do better tax planning.

We know they need to see you every quarter to make sure you pay the least amount in taxes. Of course, we hope you let us do your taxes, but I do not want that minor job to stand in the way of you getting help with your $2-million goal.

We can start small, maybe as a part-time advisor, or maybe outsourcing your bookkeeping function. This might give each of us a chance to get to know each other. I am sure you are curious if I can help you get to $2-million.

I know I am curious if you are a "Yes, and___" or "Yes, if" or "Yes, but ___" type contractor.

Focusing on the 80/20 rule to pick out future customers and services is critical. If you end up needing to spend money on advertising, at least we can target those 'right customers' and offer the 'right service' before you spray and pray that money blown all over the internet is going to pay off.

 But it goes beyond the right customer; we need the right advisors, managers, and tradesmen to drive revenue and profit. Getting to two million is great, but we better get 20% of that revenue to the bottom line once you get there. That only happens if you have dedicated help to make sure your jobs are on time and budget.

Once your CFO has analyzed your past results and set up reports so you can see that reporting from every job - the impact on your profit and management style will last for the rest of your life.

KEY IDEA:

Your part-time CFO will figure out where you are making money now and where you should stop wasting resources. The CFO does not have the emotional anchors that might keep you from making hard decisions. We can help you stop wasting cash on things that have no direct impact on your customers' experience. We will then advise you on building the framework that will take you to two million in revenue.

At two million, you have the cash flow to build a great team that shares your vision. With that team in place, getting to five or even ten million is simple, 'wash-rinse-repeat.'

How to Get the Biggest Impact from a contract CFO

The biggest impact a CFO can have in your business is to isolate the few things you already do that make the most money. That means laying out the results of the 80/20 research.

For my other contractors, I help them figure out how to eliminate all the tasks, customers, and employees that fall into the 80% "more trouble than they are worth" category. Within weeks, you will start having more fun at work and see your income grow faster than anything you have ever tried.

We all need help to stay focused on the one thing that does more for our business than anything else.

However, please keep in mind that the first step is to isolate where you are spending money that does not directly impact your customers' experience. If the customer won't notice the change, I'll strongly recommend you cut the expense. I don't have emotional anchors that force me to keep spending money where it does little good.

After cutting expenses, my other contractors had less worry and more focus. That makes it easy to focus on the one type of work, one part of town, or one type of customer they liked the most. Then they focus on that 'one thing.'

That does not mean you can only do bathroom remodels or steel buildings on farms. It could mean you focus on home remodeling in the Brookhaven area. How narrow you make your niche is up to you, but you should base the decisions on past successes.

After you get help to figure out your sweet spot, customer type, or job type, that becomes the minimum standards you will accept on future bids.

With the minimum standard fixed in your mind and written into your business plan, you can focus on building a team that will make you the preeminent builder in that segment. The entire process should take less than a month.

CHAPTER 7:
HOW MY CONTRACTOR LEFT $2.5 MILLION ON THE TABLE AND WHY HIS MISTAKE WILL LEAD YOU TO AN ALL REFERRAL BUSINESS.

O ver the past thirty years, I have hired seventeen contractors to do everything, from adding a deck for $5,000 to building two custom homes for my family on lots that I owned. One was in the $750,000 range; the second went over one million.

Do you know that NOT ONE of those 17 contractors ever called me later to see how I liked the job? No birthday cards and no request for referrals, and not a single one-to-one touch. Seventeen different builders over thirty years. You would at least think the contractor would bug me for referrals, but not a peep.

If the first builder back in 1992 had taken the time to keep in touch, he would have sold me 17 jobs for over $2.5 million. I liked the crew and the work they did, and I would have gladly kept using them. But all he got was a $5,000 deck.

In 1992, he spent the advertising dollars (in the yellow pages back then); he made the bid that included drawing up some rough samples of what my new deck would look like, and he got the deal signed. He spent a lot of time and money to gain me as a customer. But he never took the effort to talk to me again, and by the time I was ready to spend $45,000 to finish out my basement in 1995, I had forgotten his name and went somewhere else. As John Wayne was fond of saying, "Well, that's just plum nuts."

People who buy construction or home repair services never seem to do it only once; building must be addicting. So, keep in touch with your last job to get the next one. Remember, your average customer will build 2 to 5 times over the next seven years. You have invested a bundle in acquiring the first-time customer, and you will lose all that future revenue if you don't follow the lessons in this chapter.

So what is the one secret you must know?

When I've analyzed other firms' clients and jobs—here is what I found. Most of the "top-20%-projects" the contractors completed, the ones with the highest profits and happiest customers, were repeat and referral deals, **which is critical information.**

The most successful contractors are working on repeat and referral customers almost exclusively. They don't have time to bid for jobs that came in from the internet. A solid group of current customers will bring you all the business you want.

Our best future buyers are our past buyers. So why are we not friends with every 'good' customer we've ever had? If you build out a pool and deck for a customer and get invited to the celebration BBQ that shows off that pool, you will leave that party with your next job.

Is your CFO the right person to put referral and repeat sales systems in place? Everyone knows an accountant cannot sell their way out of a wet sack. It is possible that, as a trade, we are the worst salespeople ever born. However, we know how to do three things: track, measure, and analyze.

Indeed, the CFO is not your go-to person for marketing. But, we have a process that helps you create an all referral business. Three critical steps, with the third one being the most important.

1. Set up CRM (customer relationship manager) software that will force you to keep in touch with your past customers. Leading to repeat and referral business.
2. Identify and push you toward your best build and your best customer.
3. Set up an NPS tracking system, so you have the happiest customers in Atlanta.

NPS: Introducing the most impactful referral tool you've ever seen.

The NPS, which stands for (Net Promoter Score©). NPS is a simple survey tool that determines if your customers like you enough to hire you again. It tells you upfront if your customers are likely to refer you to their friends. It is a critical management tool to build an all referral business. It gives you confidence in your foreman when you can't be on every job site.

You have already seen this survey, and you probably get asked this question all the time. So here is an example of what it looks like. You may want to put a second question on the form and ask why the customer gave you that score.

You can learn a lot from an answer written in a sentence format unless it comes in two words. (I'll let you guess what the two words are.)

A simple question will tell you how your team is doing on the job site. Remember, people forget the price they paid quickly, but they remember the experience for a lifetime.

> *"Net Promoter®, NPS®, NPS Prism®, and the NPS-related emoticons are registered trademarks of Bain & Company, Inc., Satmetrix Systems, Inc., and Fred Reichheld. Net Promoter Score^SM and Net Promoter System^SM are service marks of Bain & Company, Inc., Satmetrix Systems, Inc., and Fred Reichheld."*

The NPS does not show up in your accounting software. It is a measurement system to determine how likely your current customers are to refer you to new customers. The higher the score, the more repeat and referral business you will get with higher margins. Referral business is not price-driven.

If a customer is happy, they will give you a higher NPS score.

A high score means your customer is probably going to buy from you again. The average customer will build two to five more times over the next seven years, and construction buyers never seem to stop building.

Once you have identified a buyer, do the bro-romance because that customer, if handled properly, will have a major impact on getting to $2-million. That future business should go to you, and it also means that you should generate one to three new customers by referral from those same customers.

Repeat and referral jobs are easier to manage, and you do not need to bid "bones" to get them on the jobs board. The higher your NPS score, the less you need to spend on advertising...if you need to advertise at all. I'm hoping you don't.

What do the scores mean?

If you get a score of 9 or 10, you can classify the client as a "promoter," hence the "Net Promoter Score." The promoters are enthusiastic about your business; this is where you will get 80% of your referrals. These are your most likely repeat buyers. These are the customers who will drive your business to $2-million in revenue, so you should invest in keeping them happy.

The second group will rate you in the 7 to 8 range. I call these passives. They are primarily satisfied with you, but their referral rate will be one-half of the "promoter" category. The repeat business will be dicey with this group and require you to invest a lot of effort to get the next job. However, most passives can be promoters with personal attention.

The third group is the business killer. If you get a rating of 0 to 6, the truth is they dislike you. These people post critical reviews on Yelp and spend a lot of time complaining about you to their friends.

You will not get an even spread over the survey. Some of our contractors will get 80% of their customers to give them a "promoter" score, while another 10% will fall into the 7 or 8 range, and maybe 10% will hit the 0 to 6 business-killer level of satisfaction.

The NPS score is the best indicator that you are creating happy repeat and referral customers, and it is the best indicator that you are messing up.

Here is the good news: you will not wait until you finish a job to do this survey.

I recommend you have a simple postcard (with a 1st class stamp already on the card) made up with the 0 to 10 scale and a place to write one or two sentences about the service. The foreman can hand this card to your customer every week during the job. The foreman can say, "My boss wants to make sure I am doing the right job for you. Will you fill this in and drop it in the mail?"

People love to share their opinion, so the cards come back and are pinned to the job board, so everyone knows where you stand with this customer.

If the postcard does not come back in the next day or two, follow up and ask again, or check to ensure the foreman followed directions.

Your salesman can even make this card a big deal in the bidding process. Give the customer the first postcard during the bidding process. Have the salesman tell them that the owner looks at every card during the entire building process because he wants to make sure the customer is happy with the company throughout the job.

HUMAN ENGINEERING TIP: The foreman might be scared to leave the postcard because the crew had a tough week on the job. As the owner, you must address missing cards and belay the foreman's fears. Let him know it is normal for things to go wrong. What makes your business different is how you make it right. But you can't make it right if you don't know about it.

Here is something interesting about the customer. If the crew screws up and the company makes it right, it will impress the customer. They will know you are not a "normal contractor" that does a hit-and-run. The customer with a solved problem will become your BIGGEST promoter. Mad customers made happy become referral kings.

How to Use NPS to Drive Your Company to $2-Million a year in Revenue

We want to see if 80% of your customers give you a 9 or 10 rating with NPS scores. And we want those high ratings coming from people whose profile fits our definition of the "right customer." For the rest of your life, you want these promoters to think about you as often as possible.

HUMAN ENGINEERING TIP: We recommend the owner, salesperson, or foreman make a big deal about high scores. If you make the customer feel good about saying nice things about the business, that will become the customer's mental script, and they will keep saying nice things for years.

It is okay to come right out and ask if they know anyone else that might want to build. The answer is probably no, but you have given the customer a way to thank you beyond money, which will be at the top of their mind in the future. That is how you get referrals.

An all referral business is a lot easier than you think. Customers hate buying off the internet because, in their mind, everyone is a scam. Customers want to work with trusted builders.

Your customer has an emotional desire to share you when they show off your work to their friends, and let's capitalize on that.

You must build a system of pleasant touches for your promoters. I have seen contractors call ahead when they are in the area to ask if they can stop in and check the hinges to make sure everything is working right or drop off a furniture scuff kit in case the kids hit the new kitchen cabinets with the skateboard.

This type of follow-up is something that you should put into a checklist or on the calendar in your CRM (customer relationship management) system, or you would forget to do it. It does not need to be often, maybe every six months.

It is during these calls that you uncover the next job or referral. Do not miss the opportunity to remind the customer of the great crew you have and that you would like more work.

A customer only has so much money; every business is trying to get it. So your in competition with the car and boat dealer as well as the vacation in Hawaii. But if you are in touch, the customer will skip Hawaii and build onto their house.

Use a CRM to keep in touch with everyone you meet. If you do not have CRM software in place, let the CFO figure out the most cost-effective way to keep a list of your customers, the people you did not sell, and the ones you want to bid on in the future. I call this your house-list, and it is the source of the two million you'll be bringing in from now on.

Your salesman will know what to send out or say or do regularly with all your contacts. But for goodness' sake, do not do a hit-and-run; otherwise, you will never get to $2-million.

So, keep in touch with your promoters, and your business will prosper, but what about the other two categories?

The "passive" group needs the owner's attention as well. Most of these people can go to promoter status, especially if they fit into your "right customer" profile. The only way to figure it out is to stop by and talk to them. Ask them directly: "What do we need to do to make this job perfect for you?"

Make notes and post those notes to your job board. Sometimes it may include a few hundred bucks of hard cost on your part to bring a job up to snuff in the customer's eyes. It may not even be fair that you had to do the little extra that was not in the bid. Not fair, but smart because you are on track for repeat and referral deals when you 'make it right.'

Remember, you are building 100 loyal promoters, and they will buy again and refer to others.

What about the business killer group? First, you need to know that around 10% of the people who don't like you don't like anyone else, either. They will never be happy, and they are uptight as a wet boot. As you get better at understanding your 80/20 rules for picking the right customer, you will weed most of these people out during the bidding process. It is OK to turn down an order if you have a bad feeling about the client.

I know, turning down revenue when you are trying to get to $2-million is a tough bite to chew. But you will be happier in the long run if you follow the guidelines your CFO gave you for picking out future promoters and leaving the business killers for your competitor.

Funny, but don't try this at home. A few years ago, one of my contractor clients lost his girlfriend to another builder in town. My client was pretty unhappy about it. Now in the meantime, he had already decided to stop taking bad jobs right out of the gate. From the years of experience, he knew what a bad job sounded like during the bid process. So if he could see the customer was going to be nothing but trouble, he would give them the business card of that guy that he was mad at, saying, "I'm not able to do this job, but call this guy, your right up his alley."

When you get trapped by the 0 to 6 NPS score customer, your best outcome is to fix their problem and turn them into a 10. Remember, when you make a mad customer happy, they become referral kings.

If you cannot make them happy, your next step is to keep them off Yelp and stop them from talking about your firm. Make sure the CFO sees the notes from the bad customer to improve your "right customer" list and how you select who you add. That task will move to the marketing manager when you get to the point you can afford one.

Many times, a mad customer is a job we should not have taken. Your notes will help you remember when the next jerk calls. Believe me; you will have a lot of jerks looking for you because their last builder wants nothing to do with them.

HUMAN ENGINEERING TIP: Customers who come in by referral are friends of your old customer. That's important because people associate with people who are most like themselves.

If your old customer is a nice guy, his friends are going to be nice guys. This one fact will keep most jerks out of your new customer pipeline. Plus, your old customer will push their friend into having a positive relationship.

Your old customer has an emotionally vested interest in their referrals working out for both parties. That is good for you and will lead to more 9 and 10 NPS scores.

Everyone on Payroll Is Responsible for High NPS Scores (or They Must Leave)

When you hire a foreman, you expect that foreman to operate his crew at a profit.

If that team costs you $200,000 a year, they need to bring in $600,000 of billing and net $120,000 after all costs (including the foreman's salary). The net must also include overhead allocations, like marketing, equipment, rent, and accounting.

That foreman must bring in more money than he costs, and you need to know every week if that is happening. You cannot assume anything if you want to hit $2-million at 20%.

That is an easy decision. But here is the critical information behind it:

The foreman needs to hear about the NPS score from the CFO and understand he is the biggest part of the equation. The NPS score comes from the construction team. If you have a team generating low scores, you need to step in and take remedial action.

The good news is if the foreman is aware of the number, he will self-manage the problems and get the customer to where they are likely to recommend your firm, even to their mother. If the score remains low with a particular customer, you better get in the truck and find out why. The ultimate responsibility for a high NPS score belongs to the owner.

Everyone in your business has a stake in the NPS number, and they should all have access to the reports by the team and the customer.

The entire team affects how happy your customers are. From the person who answers the phone to the clerk who bills/changes orders to the salesperson who signed the contract.

You may even decide to give everyone a $100 bonus on every job if the NPS score comes in at 9 or 10. Humans do what they get rewarded for—so let's get the entire team thinking about happy customers.

KEY IDEA:

The most financially successful firm brings in almost all of its business by referral and repeat orders. These deals are not looking for the lowest cost; they are looking for quality work.

The best tool you can use is the NPS survey to determine if your builds bring happiness to your customers. Happy customers refer to their friends.

Use CRM software to track your contact points with customers and prospects. Most future sales are lost because we don't keep in touch with the client.

CHAPTER 8:
THE SIX WAYS A CONTRACTOR CAN GROW, AND WHY A CFO WILL MAKE IT EASIER.

Whoever manages the marketing function of your business will ultimately take what the CFO has uncovered on the NPS score and the 80/20 analysis and turn it into an action plan. They will also take over the CRM system to keep in touch with all your contacts.

You may not be able to afford a marketing person today, but they will be an essential part of your two million dollar team, so keep looking for who you would like to steal away from another builder.

For smaller firms, the marketing person will run the production at the same time. You might hate this, but you cannot hire everyone you need on your $2-million team on the first day, and you probably do not have enough in reserve cash to make that kind of rash hiring decision. Your CFO knows you need a marketing person, so they will work toward making it affordable as soon as possible.

As my mother used to say: "You have waited years to get rich. A few more will not kill you."

For now, with a remote CFO on your team, you do not need to worry about the back office, so you will have enough time to hustle the business in and run the crew that gets the work done. Not worrying about the day-to-day money problems and knowing your business is building a laser-like focus on getting to $2-million will make it easier to sleep at night.

Because the CFO can track, measure, and analyze who your "right customer" is and set up the NPS system for your business, you are going to nail the first three ways to build your business:

1. Upselling your current customers (known as change orders or add-ons).

2. Selling additional jobs over the next few decades to those customers who think you are the best.

3. Generating a steady flow of referrals from those same (high NPS) clients.

But there are other methods of building a two-million-dollar firm we should review.

1. Developing a partnership/lead source for multiple repeat jobs in a category you are famous for delivering top-notch outcomes.

2. Government contracts

3. Advertising to the public (I hope you do not need to advertise.)

So, let's review the second half of the list of strategic ways to build your business.

Partnerships and Affiliate Relationships

Remember from your childhood how the Sears stores used to sell siding? They were maniacs in the '60s and '70s with their TV campaigns that all ended with the tagline: Installation by a Sears trained and approved licensed contractor.

At one time, thousands of contractors all over America were willing to trade a portion of their gross revenues for a steady flow of contracts—all involving the same work. Doing the same thing every day made it easier for the contractor to hire tradesmen and control quality. Sears paid the contractor, so all the local guys had to do was get the crew on the job site and start building.

Even today, there are other opportunities like the Sears siding deal. If you want to take away many of the headaches of owning a business, your CFO can stay on the lookout for deals like this one.

A Twenty-one-year-old Army Brat Nails the 1% With an Exclusive Relationship

Two years ago, I met Carol, a CPA from Nashville, while attending a tax planning seminar. She started telling me about her new client, "Jeff," a twenty-one-year-old who was fresh out of welding school and making almost **$5,000** a week in net profit. WOW! For West Tennessee, he was already close to the 1% at such a young age. I wanted to hear more.

The CPA told me that Jeff got a job three days after graduating from the junior college welding program in May. The job offer was a good one: $24 an hour erecting steel buildings on farms in West Tennessee. Jeff jumped on the offer and loved it.

In two months, he had put up five buildings as part of a six-man crew. The guy who had the erection contract with the building manufacturer in Jackson was a skilled human engineer and got a lot of work done fast.

But then it all went upside down.

The crew was in Memphis about 150 miles from home when the contractor's wife drove onto the job site one afternoon screaming about a tax lien. The IRS had cleared out the bank accounts and locked up the shop. It seemed Jeff's boss had been ignoring the letters for a few years now.

The boss came around and said, "Boys, we are busted. I am leaving with my wife, and we are moving out to her sister's place in Oklahoma. All I have on me is enough to give each of you $100 for gas money to get back home. I am sorry."

With that, the good job walked off the site, and the crew was left stunned.

That is everyone except the farmer who needed the building, and he was panicking.

He had called the manufacturer, and the best they could do was another crew out there in November because they were behind.

The farmer came around and said, "If you boys will stay on this job and finish it, I will pay you $30 an hour in cash right here on the barrelhead at the end of every day. I have got to have this building up right now, or I will have hay sitting on the ground when the snow hits."

Jeff and the other boys picked up their welding gloves and finished the building. Did a fine job, and the farmer was true to his word. They got paid cash every night. On Thursday, they finished, and everyone packed up to go back to Nashville to look for another job. That is everyone but Jeff. He drove to Jackson that night because he had an idea that the manufacturer may need another erection contractor.

Jeff walked into the headquarters the next morning. He offered to erect steel buildings all over West Tennessee if the factory could finagle a way around the contractor's license, insurance, and all the other details of running a business.

The factory had fifty back-orders for installation and was happy to have a way out of the problem. They had numerous details, and I am not sure if they did not skip more than one local building ordinance in the first few months. But Jeff was no longer a welder; he was now a business owner.

Jeff called the other five guys over the weekend, offered to hire them all back, and threw in a few perks.

"First," he said, "We are going to work three days a week, not five. We will drive out to the job site on Sunday evening in two pickups and a tool trailer. On Monday at 5 a.m., we will start building, even if we need to use floodlights, and we will work until 9 p.m. We will erect that building in 72 hours."

One of the other guys said, "My daddy called that 'caint to caint.' Working from when you cannot see in the morning until you cannot see at night."

Jeff continued, "If we get that farmer to sign off on the job ticket at 9 p.m. on Wednesday, not only do you get the $24 an hour, but I am also going to throw in another $300 bonus. We will camp on the job site, eat out of the cooler, and shower when we get back home. No drugs, drinking, or womenbing.. We are there to build and scoot. Then you will have four days off before we head out again."

All this from a twenty-one-year-old kid. Obviously, being an Army brat his whole life, some of that organization skill he saw had rubbed off on Jeff.

My CPA friend told me that Jeff had hired her accounting firm to get all the paperwork for payroll, contractors' licensing, and insurance. The manufacturer had agreed to let Jeff use their license—but only for a few months. So, Jeff needed someone to handle the details while he ran the crew.

Carol was even making sure that a local dirt contractor had leveled the lot and poured the footings the week before. That was outside the parameters of being an accountant, but Carol was excited to be part of this kid's vision.

People are naturally drawn to 'Yes, and ___' types of people. Even the accountant was going out of her way to help.

The factory had the steel building on a flatbed sitting on the farm on Sunday afternoon, and they brought a forklift to pick up the beams on Monday morning before the truck went back to the factory. Jeff knew how to get the project done fast and with a crew that had done it before.

In one weekend, using someone else's customers, Jeff built a construction business out of nothing and pulled $5,000 a week to the bottom line.

The factory was so impressed that Jeff had figured out how to assembly-line-build, they promised him fifty-two jobs a year. But Jeff dialed it back for the opening week of deer season and Christmas with his mom and dad.

What impressed the CPA was that Jeff put himself on the same payroll as his five friends, about $1,400 a week. The other $3,600 in profits were going into his investment fund from day one. He never talked about the profits with anyone except his CPA and his parents. He did not buy a new truck; he played the poor country boy like a fiddle. Jeff was probably going to be rich by the time he was twenty-five.

This type of thinking is behind every excellent construction business. If you are building something different every month, everything is a one-off task, and you spend a lot of time figuring it out and training and teaching your team how to get it done.

Now it was plain luck that Jeff was in the right place at the right time. However, there are many opportunities like the Sears Siding and steel farm buildings in the market.

Home Depot and Lowes offer affiliated contractors to their customers every day. They even pay the sales assistant a $100 spiff (and give them an award called a "Homer.") whenever they bring a buyer to the front of the store.

I tell the companies I work with that if it fits after we do our 80/20 analysis and figure out the "right customer," they may want us to get on these approved contractor lists.

Why do you not have something like this going on already? When you are busy, you concentrate on everything urgent and do not have time for what's important. It happens to everyone in the business.

With a CFO on your team who understands your vision, they can start looking for deals like Jeff's. They can make the inquiry calls and even help you negotiate the deal at a rate that would not bust you. Sometimes we hear from another contractor about these types of opportunities and may be able to pass them on to you. That's another reason a construction specialist is so important.

Now, a third-party referral project rarely happens as quickly as Jeff pulled it off.

For the first few weeks, your CFO will be busy getting your ducks in a row, so you have a path to $2-million. But when the dust clears, we will bring this idea up again and start looking for referral contracts if it fits your model.

Government Contracts

You have probably thought about government contracts but never got around to getting on the list. You may have looked at the pre-qualifications and decided that was way over your pay grade. Well, let me tell you about my neighbor and what happened to him.

About five years ago, my sixty-four-year-old neighbor, "Ernie," announced that he was selling his dirt-moving business to his employees and moving to a house in Brookhaven. I was shocked;

he drove a five-year-old pickup and wore jeans to work every day. Ernie was about the nicest guy you would ever want to meet, always telling jokes and acting like he stole the last piece of cherry pie.

How in the world can you afford to buy a $3 million house, I asked?

He smiled and explained that about twenty years ago, he got a government contract to work on a section of road that was so far out of town, nobody wanted to bid on the job. His wife (who passed away from cancer last year) had been doing a lot of work in the background to get their small company approved for government contracts. When they finally landed one, it was a watershed moment.

Ernie told me that "since that country road project, I have been at full speed every month for the past twenty years. Now, I can retire. I am only sorry my wife cannot be here to join me on the golf course."

But I was not done with my questions. "How can you make so much money off these contracts? I thought they were all bid at dog bone pricing?"

"So did I," Ernie replied. "I am glad my wife found out differently. They do not pay quickly. We had to get help from our accountant to borrow enough to cover overhead between draws, and we needed to qualify for leases on new equipment, and I had to hire that out to an accounting firm because we could not do Excel that well.

"But once you have the cash flow budget figured out, it is pretty profitable. The big advantage is you know a year in advance where and when you will work next. Fixing old roads is a long-term project unless the Feds decide to drop a billion on Georgia for infrastructure, then they go a lot quicker. But the billion-dollar infrastructure deal only seems to happen at election time."

He explained, "We had to learn how to manage the inspectors. Several times, they would send out college kids to tell us how to build. We had to learn how not to anger them while explaining what we were doing.

"Oh, and one more thing, the employment regulations are so cumbersome that we eventually had to hire a CFO to manage the details and keep our budget up to date. That is one thing I wish we would have done right from the beginning. My wife lost a lot of sleep trying to do money-things that were way over her head and mine too."

Now you may want to move into government contracting as well. The cities around Atlanta and the rest of the state are looking for bids every month, and they have set aside jobs for small contractors that you could grab.

Here, Ernie applied with the Georgia Department of Transportation and had a slew of hoops and paperwork before he could even do the little backcountry road job. But once he had that nailed, he became approved by all the municipalities and school districts within 50 miles of his shop.

You can find the list of hoops on the Georgia DOT web page titled "Contractor Prequalification."

One of the critical requirements is audited financials and budgets. Then you need to bid on those jobs, which means you need to understand the cost, or you'll suffer.

Here is a kicker that you need to know about: we are CPAs offering to be your part-time offsite CFO. However, since we are on the inside, we cannot provide the audits the Georgia DOT and others will require because of conflict-of-interest rules. We will, however, find the best deal for you from another firm here in the Atlanta area so you can deliver your audit reports with your bids.

Getting you qualified for government work, finding the bids that fit your business, and then getting the bids in on time is something a part-time CFO can do. If you win the bid, we will work on a line of credit to carry you between draws and get the financing you need for equipment. It is a big opportunity, but it requires an experienced hand to bring it all together.

Advertising

You have already figured out that we are not fans of advertising to generate sales leads as a business strategy. It should be last on your list, not first, if you want to find quality customers.

It is not uncommon to get so wrapped up in online marketing that you lose your common sense. Every day we hear about how the new online world will bring in a flood of quality clients at a buck apiece. There must be 10,000 so-called gurus telling you how easy it is to get rich.

But all these guys are the same one-trick-pony. They get the phone to ring a dozen times a day, and then it is up to you to sort out the "right customers" from all the calls. That is generally poor use of your time, but it is all they have. On the inside, they call it to spray and pray. With all that said, there is a caveat. Suppose you do not have one hundred happy customers on your books.

In that case, you may need to advertise eventually because ten or twenty satisfied customers are not enough to referral and repeat your way to $2-million.

BUT don't expand your cold client advertising until you have implemented the right customer 80/20 rule analysis. Do not waste money getting new customers unless 80% of your current customers give you a 9 to 10 rating on the NPS score sheet. Do not start looking for new customers until you have exhausted the other five ways a contractor can build their firm.

Some of those six business-building ideas don't fit your situation. You may throw out ideas like government contracting or working for a steel building manufacturer, which is okay, and I put them in here to get you thinking about what is possible.

Spending money before the basic steps are in the bag will lead to more chaos but not more net profit. That is because you cannot control the quality of the lead when you are advertising. You will need to deal with a lot of junk—and that can eat at your soul and cash flow.

NOTE: You will need a friendly website and social media presence.

Here is a secret on how to get the most bang for your buck: Instead of 100 pages of pictures and other content, post 90-second video clips of your current customers talking about you in front of the project you recently completed. You can use your phone to capture the video, and the more amateurish the recording, the more believable it is.

When a referral wants to look you up on the internet before calling, they are not looking for pictures of Atlanta skyscrapers or Better Homes and Gardens style houses. They want to know who you are, and they want to know you have built what they need for other happy customers.

NOTE: Advertising is outside the scope of a CFO, but we are great at sifting through the pitches you will hear and tracking the results of any advertising you do end up buying in real-time. All of us have wasted tens of thousands of dollars on advertising that was not well-planned and not targeted to your key customer. We will keep those proposals off your desk.

Advertising Best Practices

Like everything you do In business, advertising requires tracking, measuring, and analyzing, and that's what a CFO was born to do.

A few years ago, I read a book by the late Gary Halbert. He was one of the most famous ad writers in American history, and his copy has generated billions in sales for the people lucky enough to hire him.

Until I read his book, I always thought those guys who can write a clever sales letter or TV commercial must be the most ingenious people on the planet. What I learned in his book took that esteem down about thirty notches until I finally understood the brilliance behind effective advertising.

Halbert explained that when he was selling anything new, he first looked at what everyone else was doing in the niche and then stole the top five to ten ideas and put them on a big whiteboard.

He then added fifty to one hundred of his ideas on how to get the customer to buy. He threw everything he could think of on the wall to see what would stick. After boiling it down to a dozen ideas, he did small test runs to see which ideas had any merit in the customer's eyes. Halbert knew it did not matter what he thought was good or bad; it was what the customer thought that counted.

Then he started revising based on results. He ran small newspaper ads or sent out two hundred letters to see if his advertising copy got any traction. (This was before the Internet.) When he found a winner, he started expanding on what worked.

How did he decide what was a winner or not?

Gary never started the project without a tracking system and analysis spreadsheet already in place. He threw everything against the wall and measured what worked.

That is the work that a CFO does. We track everything and analyze it to see what works. Gary was not a genius; he was an accountant.

Here is why this is important to you. When you get a call from someone saying we can find leads from this or that; you must ask them a specific question:

"I am a contractor that specializes in backyard decks. My customer is a homeowner who lives in a 2,500 to a 5,000-square-foot house who wants a nicer backyard. Have you done that type of lead generation for anyone else in a different city? And, since they would be in a non-competing market, I would like to talk to those contractors to see how qualified the leads are, okay?"

Here is what you are going to hear about 99% of the time:

"We can target that customer by doing search engines, and I am positive we can find the right ad to pull in those prospects."

But he does not know who you are or what you sell. He did not research your business before calling. They do not have a track record of solving your problem, but they hope you will be the first. The customer you are looking for is not identifiable by them, but hopefully, they will figure it out because deck buyers will search on Google. They do not know what ad will work. You will hire them to throw a bunch of mud on the wall to see if they can figure out something. Oh, and one more thing, you will pay them $2,000 to $5,000 a month for their brilliance while they test a bunch of unproven ideas in Atlanta.

As a CFO, I must keep you out of chaos. That kind of lead generation sounds like thin ice on a hot day.

Is a CFO (Or any accounting help) an Expense or an Investment?

For most contractors, buying accounting is a giant waste of money, just like insurance.

The truth is, if we were not afraid of getting sued, we would skip insurance, and if we did not think the IRS would put us in jail, we would skip accounting as well. To nine out of ten business owners, accounting is a black hole with no ROI, which is plum nuts.

The black hole reputation is something my industry deserves. We take numbers off invoices and checks and put them into little boxes on a computer screen to generate reports. We then take the numbers out of those reports and put them into more little boxes to do your tax return.

It takes a lot of skill to know what goes where and a lot of guesses to figure out your intentions when you moved money, telling no one why. But the bottom line for the average accounting firm or bookkeeper, we are simply skilled clerks.

Watching Janet crying in the hallway at the QuickBooks seminar changed all that for me.

I decided I would no longer be the "average accountant."

I have seen firsthand what makes a construction business successful. I know how to get you to $2-million, the base number you must have to be a proper business.

I know your future success is in your current numbers, and you only need to dig out a few critical insights and then focus your energy on the winners. But you need the courage to get rid of the projects and people dragging you down.

I have helped others to the next level and hope this book will help you do the same.

When you engage our accounting firm at the remote CFO level, we start with the 80/20 analysis of the business. That makes it possible for you to pinpoint who your "right customer" is.

Then we look for ways to slash $1,000 a week out of your operating expenses without affecting the customer's experience because we do not want you to have negative cash flow, or you may tire of us quickly.

Whenever a contractor takes a giant step that involves expanding overhead, we know you will be second-guessing your decision every day for at least six months.

I hope to dispel those fears in the first four weeks by figuring out how to squeak out my pay with cost-cutting. Then to drive more net profits by focusing on the "right customer." So, I need to hit the ground like a jackrabbit with a coyote on its tail.

Within a few weeks, we will be ready to make the first significant strategic improvements toward driving your business to the $2-million levels. That's when I will start doing the NPS analysis. After we have a clear path to victory, we will look at each of the six ways a contractor can build sales.

CHAPTER 9:
CREATING WEALTH
FROM YOUR BUSINESS.

About sixty years ago, when my uncle was young, he ran a trash hauling business out of the back of his 3100 Chevy pickup.

Every Saturday, he drove around our community and dropped off empty 50-gallon barrels in the alley. He then picked up the old ones full of ashes. There was no EPA in 1961, and everyone burned their trash in a barrel in the alley right after dinner. He told me that the air hung heavy with the smell of soot and ash on a still night.

Now, Uncle Jr. ran the business in cash. His record-keeping was on a pocket-sized spiral notepad he kept in the front pocket of his overalls, and his bank account was a sock full of cash that he kept tucked in his underwear. (That may have been too much information.)

When he got home on Saturday night, my aunt made him shower outside with the garden hose before he could come in the house for supper. It was dirty work.

He did well for the times because no one else wanted the dirty job. His profit margins were in the 70% range, and he never worried about taxes or regulations. It was a simple time to be in business.

These days, in every business, margins are razor thin, competitors are everywhere, and the government thinks you are a bottomless pit of tax revenue. And no matter how many regulations they dump on you, they believe you will be their little cash cow forever. Life is not so simple anymore.

Today, a contractor needs to make the right decision about jobs they take, billing in progress, and their labor utilization rates. Uncle Jr. would be lost today.

Create Wealth—Not Income

In construction, you have two sources of wealth:

1. What you take out of the business and move to your investment funds.
2. What you sell the business for when you're done.

Scrape off the top and move it to your investment account

As the owner, you must see a path to wealth, or you will tire of being the boss. No business prospers if it does not meet the needs of the owner first. That may sound selfish, and it sure does not fit the mamby-pamby feel-good attitude that we see on TV about "giving back."

But the bottom line is, if you are not creating wealth, you will get tired and start taking half measures. You will start wondering if you can get by on "half a tank" of gas.

I believe we should be a force for good in our community – but I also believe in making a profit. Poor business owners cannot "give back." You must meet your needs first. However, I hope your needs don't include new Cadillacs and diamond rings. If you're attracted to shiny objects, wealth is hard to come by.

My job is to make sure you are operating above 80% of your potential at all times and are driven to cross the finish line first. I believe in the profit-first philosophy that you should scrape your income off the top upfront. Then let your team figure out how to meet the company goals with whatever money is left.

I hope you can set yourself up on a modest monthly salary somewhere between $6,000 and $10,000 a month. That's not in stone; it's just the average for my other clients.

I understand that family comes first, so we do not want to ask for any sacrifices at home so you can hit $2-million. I also appreciate the recommended monthly salary is not enough to buy everything you want.

When I first started making money, my dad gave me some brilliant advice when he caught me looking over my shoulder at a brand new Platinum F-350. He said, "It makes no difference how much you make; it's how much you keep that sets us apart." Accumulating wealth is a lot easier if you are not worried about your $1,100 truck payment. And keep in mind that austerity is not forever.

At two million in revenue, you could drop $20,000 to $35,000 a month to the bottom line. When you hit that kind of income, I'm hoping you put every dime of extra profit into your investment portfolio. Pull it out of the company fast; if you leave a big chunk of cash on hand, you do not act hungry. Remember, a lean dog runs fast.

With consistency, there is a good chance that you will probably make more money from your investments than your construction business in five to ten years. My definition of being rich is the day your investment income matches your work income; on that day, work becomes optional.

I have seen carpenters making $46,000 a year who were rich. I have had contractors taking $600,000 a year out of their business, and the slightest bump would put them into default and panic. You never want to hear that old Georgia saying, "that boy is all hat, and no cattle."

Building wealth gives you a cushion when this boom runs out, and it will run out. Anyone who remembers listening to the Beatles on AM radio will tell you, *'boom times, yep, I have seen this before, and it is going to end just like the others.'*

HUMAN ENGINEERING TIP: When you are "rich," it changes you emotionally. You no longer live with the fear that you cannot make payroll on Friday or pay the kids' tuition at the private school. That means when you get a "business-killer" NPS score from a customer, you know you can walk away from the chaos, and everything will be just fine. You have the confidence to stick to your bids and just say no when it's the right long-term decision.

You have the sleep of the angels and wake up every morning refreshed and happy to conquer the new problems you will receive today. Rich people who earned their money honestly are the happiest people I know, and you are joining their ranks in the next few years.

Profiting From Selling a Successful Business

The second way you will get rich is by selling your business. A well-run company with a solid customer base and a good crew is in high demand, especially if some national contractor wants to expand to Atlanta to take advantage of our business climate. You must always be ready to sell, or you might miss your chance.

The secret to "being ready" is implementing the processes I have outlined in this book. That includes a cash management process, a crackerjack workflow system, and a referral and repeat client acquisition plan.

I also recommend that we do a business valuation once a year when we do your tax returns. It is a great ego booster and gives you an insight into the value you are creating. If your business is worth $200,000 more at the end of next year, it is a mental boost. By the way, you should only share that information with your mom and your wife because no one else will be happy for you except your CFO.

I do not anticipate shopping your business to potential buyers, and it is better to be famous and have the buyer call us. But if you decide you want to list it for sale in the future, I will visit the brokers in town, explain my valuation to them, and bring you my recommendations on the best way to sell.

Remember, a well-run operation doing $2-million with a path to $10-million is worth a lot more. So if you can wait to sell, it will be better in the long run.

How to make your business valuable

Buyers are looking for cash flow, your connections, your systems, and your employees. Generally, they are not that interested in your equipment. So building a profitable business with good customers and staff is where you should focus your energies.

With a CFO on your team, the owner will always know where they are making a profit and what they need to create systems that reduce chaos and cost. One of our first-year goals will be to ensure that the bookkeeping is accurate, that all the jobs are costed out correctly, and that customers are billed for change orders. That is a lot of data.

To help, we will create a dashboard that you can review every day to put all the management information on your phone or desktop computer. It will look something like this, but not exactly because every contractor is a little different.

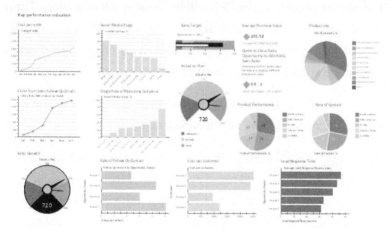

This data will tell you where you are, but it will not tell you much about where you are going. That is the second job of a part-time CFO.

Like the Johnny Carson character "Carnac the Magnificent," a CFO is your best chance of hiring a fortune teller. The CFO's big question is, "what have I seen from the past that gives me an idea of the future?" The CFO is removed from wishful thinking and unfounded optimism because their life revolves around real numbers.

Growing to $2-million will require you to make numerous changes in your staffing, workflow, and even the customers you accept from now on. It will require you to line up financing and tighten the job costing, bidding, and billing systems. The CFO will implement best practices in these areas and bring what they have learned from other contractors to your business. If the owner doesn't have to worry about such things, they will put more energy into customers.

If there are problems, the CFO will fix them or prevent them. There are no examples of a contractor growing large without a finance person on the team. In a well-run business, there are fewer crises to manage, that alone may be worth the price of admission.

Ever hear about the CPA at the old-time gas station...the kind where they ran out and serviced your car?

> The CPA was looking for some summertime work on the side, but he got fired the very first day on the job. It seems a customer pulled up to the pump and yelled out, "Fill 'er up!" The CPA looked at him for a minute, knocked on the window, and asked, "Do you think you could get by on half a tank?"

However, when you bring a "money man" onto your team, make sure your CFO is a "Yes, and ___" type of guy.

Your CFO must be of the "Yes, and ___" and "glass half full" mentality, or they will "caution" you into mediocrity. That positive attitude is rare; it comes from owning and working in several types of business, not only an accounting firm, over the years. Accountants are trained to find what's wrong or tell you what won't work. That's why many contractors are frustrated with their tax preparers.

A CFO considers all that 'what is going to fail' training but then asks, "what will work?"

If you hire a CFO who has never worked outside of accounting, he is probably like the poor guy at the gas station, a glass half empty kind of advisor, and you will never get out of your own way with that kind of team. Your CFO must be on board with your goal of getting to $2-million.

We all need an outside set of eyes to be on our side, and watch over our decisions. The bottom line is that we often get caught up in urgent problems like a load of lumber not arriving on time, a foreman showing up drunk, or a plumber breaking a pipe and flooding the house. Those minor crises keep us from thinking clearly about the important tasks that will get you to two million.

From this month forward, the important will be the job of the CFO, who will sort out the details and bring usable information every week.

Summary for creating wealth with your construction business.

By scraping a percentage of gross revenue off the top and using as little as possible to pay your living expenses – you will build an investment portfolio that will generate more income in 10 years than your business. That is your primary source for creating generational wealth.

When you create a solid business with workflow systems, a good team, and great customers, you will sell your business at five times net income, possibly more.

Now neither of these outcomes are guaranteed, but they are both the CFO's goal for you.

CHAPTER 10: FORMULATING FINANCIAL STRATEGIES FOR GROWTH

With rapid growth, cash flow dries up. The faster your business grows, the more strategic the CFO must become to ensure you do not run out of money.

You can make numerous mistakes in business and survive, but the ONE mistake you cannot make is missing payroll. Your crew will spend the weekend looking for a new job. Missing payroll is a mortal error, and on Monday, when you have no employees, you can put a fork in your business because you are finished.

The CFO will manage the money, so you stay in business long enough that the growth eventually becomes profit and shows up as positive cash flow.

Payroll is only one example. A CFO takes on the responsibility of making sure draws and deposits come in faster than expenses go out, so the owner can focus on bidding jobs and running the crew.

Line Up $100,000 to $500,000 of Credit When You *Do Not* Need It

Part of the strategic management of cash flow is lining up credit before you need it. When you have a CFO on your team, the bank or other capital sources pay attention and take you seriously. A CFO is a significant credibility factor.

You will need the credit if you land bigger jobs that are slow on the draw or deposits. You may also get a chance to buy a competitor's business or used equipment from time to time, and it will be great if you can put your hands on a few hundred thousand dollars at a moment's notice.

All bigger businesses have substantial lines of credit

There are many sources of credit besides the bank. Of course, credit and using it are two different things. But it is far better to have a credit line and not need it than to be out of cash and nowhere to turn. Planning is the wheelhouse for a CFO; it is what we do best.

During the first year as your CFO, I will work toward securing $100,000 to $500,000 of credit for the business.

Weathering the Next Downturn: Who Are You Going to Dance With, When the Music Stops?

You know in your heart that the boom will not last forever. I read the state sales tax reports every month, lumber price futures daily, and the new construction reports to keep on top of the state of the economy. It is going to change.

Since the CFO is your best fortune teller, I will keep you informed of what I see when we work together.

However, I will also start planning that you don't get caught with your Wranglers down around your boots. The first step is to make sure that your costs are variable. Now the easy one is labor. If you have no work, you can cut back on labor costs. But we should look at every cost the same way.

If you sign a bunch of loans for trucks, forklifts, and backhoes and the jobs dry up, you are still on the hook for those payments. I am going to do my best to keep you out of the fixed overhead. If we need a backhoe, I can see if we rent it or borrow from another contractor. If that does not work, we can buy a used one with some life still in it.

There is almost always a way to get what you need without committing to big monthly payments that put the company at risk. If you need to borrow money to put a $400,000 tractor into service, that tractor better run night and day.

There are many ways to keep the fixed payments as low as possible, and I will review every payment you make to find a better alternative. We know the storm is coming – we do not know when, though.

The good news for contractors is an unspoken upside: in a severe downturn, you'll be able to raise your prices.

In 2009, my neighbor painted the house he had for sale. He complained that when real estate was booming two years earlier, the bid was $3,500, and everyone was busy. One year into the recession and the best offer he could get was $5,500. Paul was a retired wealthy business owner, so he naturally asked the painting contractor about the price jump. He was curious why the bids had jumped.

The contractor explained that 75% of the painting contractors had quit the business after the 2008 recession, and the few that remained could charge a premium because there was no competition.

When the boom ends, I would love to see you in the same position as the painting contractor that worked at my neighbor's house. Fewer jobs, but you are the last man standing, so pricing is not an issue.

Buy Your Competitor and Get Their Tradesmen to Work for You

Weathering the coming storm has another upside as well.

If you have cash in the bank or a hefty line of credit, opportunities are going to pop up almost every month to buy out a competitor.

Most contractors are good at selling jobs or getting the work done, but few are good at finance and do not realize how important a "money man" is to their business.

To most, it seems prudent to have their wife do the books and run the business based on COH, cash on hand. That means a lot of contractors go out of business every year in Atlanta. In your eyes, that should spell opportunity.

If a local competitor is going under, you could buy that business for ten cents on the dollar.

The significant advantage of buying out a competitor is you get the past customer list. Remember, people who build never stop. Now you have a whole new list of future customers already sorted out.

Even better, you get the tradesmen to come to work for you. In a time when your biggest limitation on landing more jobs is finding the people to do the work, receiving a dozen or more skilled people is a Godsend.

One more tip: Whenever a contractor goes out of business, at the very least, try to buy their phone number. They left a lot of bids and business cards all over town, and for the next few years, customers are still going to call that phone.

> **HUMAN ENGINEERING TIP:** A broke contractor looks in the yard to see what equipment and supplies he has on hand and values the business based on tangible assets. It's easy to understand. In his mind, he will judge your offer against what the auctioneer offered.
>
> Panicked sellers have no idea the real value is the customer list and employee roster.
>
> I have a friend who has bought several businesses for pennies on the dollar because we split out the assets. The equipment went to auction, and we got what appeared to be a list of names for almost nothing.
>
> There is no reason I cannot show up at that auction and pick up a few pieces of equipment we need at a significant discount, as well; another reason to have pre-approved lines of credit.

Get that $400,000 tractor another way.

Around twenty years ago, "Charles" had an oil field construction project in Casper, Wyoming. He needed a four-wheel loader but could not beg, borrow, or steal one from anybody.

The Caterpillar dealer had one, but he would need at least 20% down on the $400,000, plus pay the sales tax and other ownership costs.

Charles would be locked into ownership and need to ship it back to Atlanta when the snow came.

Then he got lucky; a local auctioneer told him that the bank had a repo from a hot-shot kid who should have paid more attention to his accountant. Charles might get it cheap.

So, he went to see the bank that made the loan, and the loan officer was nervous. His annual review was approaching while the loader sat there in the parking lot of the bank. If it stayed on the non-performing loan list, it would look bad for his ratios, and his annual review would not go well.

He offered the tractor to Charles if he assumed the loan balance (about $315,000) with no down payment, back payments, or sales tax. He could start making payments and get it out of the parking today, the banker told him. With a deal like that, Charles did not mind paying the $5,500 it would cost to ship it to Atlanta when he finished this job.

So, he thought about it for a moment and said, "Okay, I will solve your problem, but I have one requirement. I want the loan on a non-recourse basis."

What "non-recourse" means is if Charles has a business downturn himself someday and cannot make the $4,000 payments, the bank can take the loader back without going through foreclosure lawsuits and other hassles, and they can just drive out and pick it up.

Also, the bank cannot come after him for the balance once they send the repo to auction, and they cannot report this as a default on his company's credit report.

The young banker looked out the window at that loader, sighed, and gave him the deal. The payments were still a fixed amount every month (which Charles hates). But if he had a downturn, he could get out of the deal.

A CFO is always on the lookout for failing competitors. They are always working toward building your credit line, so you can pull the trigger when the opportunity arises.

If you find a deal, the CFO's understanding of accounting gives you a better chance at making it a good deal.

Sales Versus Labor Cost - The Fastest Way to Tell If You Are Going to Have a Cash Flow Problem

Accounting software is for GAAP reports. That means Generally Accepted Accounting Principles.

When I close out the books at the end of the month, a big part of my job is to make sure a banker or auditor will feel good about the accuracy of those numbers.

However, there is a report that is not GAAP-approved, and it is not in your accounting software. We call it the SLC, sales versus labor cost.

In every construction business, your highest cost is payroll. If your people are working full bore, you are close to 100% labor utilization rates. You are billing for every hour you are paying an employee. That might mean that for every $4.00 of billing this week, your labor was $1.00. At a 4 to 1 ratio, you are doing good. What if that ratio changes? It is the first sign that you could have a cash flow problem in four to six weeks.

If payroll is $10,000 for the week, and you only billed $25,000, your ratio goes from 4-to-1 down to 2.5-to-1. That means you are paying way over normal for payroll, and your labor utilization rate went off a cliff.

If I see this, I know you need to take remedial steps today, or this problem will show up in your checking account in a matter of weeks.

The SLC ratio is a number that I will check every week. You must do it on a spreadsheet because it is not something most CPAs even recognize, but it is the best leading indicator of future cash flow I have ever found, right behind getting paid on time from your customers.

Grandpa Said, "Don't Make Any Mistakes."

I once asked my grandfather what his secret to business success was. He smiled and said, "That's simple. Work from 'cain't to cain't,' and only do work that the customers are paying you for. Oh, and one more thing, don't make any mistakes."

I laughed and said, "So, your best advice is not to make any mistakes. I cannot believe you are not a chess champion or something, Grandpa."

Big mistakes happen in your business: lost bids, bad employees, lawsuits, etc. We do not know what will go wrong, but I can promise you some terrible surprises are coming. If you plan – the problems won't kill you.

Our biggest mistake is that "I waited too long to _____" - fill in the blank; it's a mortal error in most cases because we do not fix a problem until we are bleeding to death. It reminds me of that old cowboy song by Tex Ritter:

> There was blood on the saddle and blood all around
> And a great big puddle of blood on the ground©

The sad part is that it's our blood. A CFO will point out the cuts while there is still time to save your life.

Our second mistake we make is the inaccurate assumption. (I know I keep repeating myself.)

What you feel, think, or hope is never the whole truth. When you have a seasoned CFO on your team, you have a second set of logical eyes on the ball, and our job is to point out the dangers of the inaccurate assumption in your decision-making or your reluctance to decide.

A good CFO is never a "yes man." We may be 'Yes and _____' but we're never 'yes boss.'

I guess you could call that being an advisor. After a few months, your CFO will know more about your business than you do. The numbers do not lie; they do not exaggerate, and they do not know what wishful thinking is.

Every business is susceptible to "groupthink" the owner comes up with an idea, and the entire team starts agreeing and clapping. That is nuts. I have told my team in the past, "If you agree with everything I say, one of us is no longer needed."

The CFO brings the logical, not the wishful, to the table. You will hear, "I know what you **want** to do, but here is what you CAN do." The bigger your business, and the faster you grow, the more danger you face from "groupthink," especially if you succeed.

Expense Controls: Stolen Gas, Flowers, and a Lap Dance

Expenses get out of control without someone riding herd on the problem

One of my contractors has a satellite office in Macon. About a year ago, a customer was going to come into that office to review the possibility of building a new warehouse.

It would be a multi-million-dollar deal. So, my client, "Peter," wanted to make a good impression. He told the office manager to order fresh flowers for the entryway to spruce up the place. The bill was probably around $50, so Peter thought nothing about it, and after he closed the deal, he drove back to Atlanta.

About four months later, Peter was going back to Macon for another meeting, and when he walked into the office, there was a fresh bouquet at the front door. "What is this?" he asked.

"Boss," the receptionist answered, "I was told to put fresh flowers in the office. We are so lucky that the local florist could put us on their route, and they deliver every Monday."

What was supposed to be a one-time event had gone on for seventeen weeks. Almost $1,000 of hard cash leaked out the door.

When people are not spending their own money, they spend a little quicker. Peter lost $1,000 because he did not have a system to monitor all the expenses coming across the bookkeeper's desk every day.

Another client was down at the shop on Sunday afternoon, loading one of the company trucks with supplies for an out-of-town job in the morning. "Carl" had recently received company credit cards that ping you every time you use them with the transaction details. Carl got a ping, and it said one of his welders had filled up the company truck at the Shell station for $87.50. The same truck that Carl was loading at that exact minute.

The ping turned out to be a big money saver. The following week, Carl got a ping at 2:30 AM from a bar with a brass pole out by the airport. The coded $150 invoice was by one of his salespeople as entertainment with a recent customer. To Carl, that sounded like the salesman was entertaining someone on his lap.

A CFO will implement best-in-class technology to track expenses. They will link those costs to a specific job for an accurate picture of the profit margins.

Most research on employees spending company money shows that 5% is waste or outright fraud. On $1-million of expenses over a year – that's $50,000. Most of the expense tracking phone apps are cheap and easy to use.

Summary

The most critical point of this chapter is to build your access to credit. It may take several years to get your credit lines to a half million, but you will need access to cash, or your growth may put you out of business.

Plan now for the bottom falling out of the construction market. It will happen; we just don't know when. Keep as much of your cost as possible in the variable column. So that you can reduce overhead before you are forced to say, "I waited too long to _____."

Watch for competitors that are failing. You may get their customer list and tradesman roster for pennies on the dollar. At the very least, try to buy their phone number because it may ring for a couple more years with opportunities from old customers.

Watch your billing vs. labor cost every week. It is the first indicator that you may suffer cash flow problems in a few weeks. This report is not in your software.

Set up controls for your expense accounts. Most research points out that around 5% of employee spending is unnecessary or outright fraud. If you are spending a million a year, you could lose $50,000.

The tips in chapter ten have to do with important tasks, not urgent ones. That is why you probably haven't gotten around to doing any of them. I'll fix it.

CHAPTER 11:
IS PAYING FOR JOB COSTING WORTH ALL THE WORK AND MONEY?

J ob costing is number five on the list of mistakes made by every construction business, and remember the secret of success, according to my grandpa: do not make any mistakes.

Last year, I had a new contractor come in. His name was "Ken," and he was fresh out of college with a degree in construction management. He passed his contractor's license exam with flying colors, and he had a bright idea to pay off his college loans quickly.

He would build a house for his mom's friend, who is looking for a builder. She had a budget of $400,000 for a 2,000-square-foot place on a half-acre out on the west side of Atlanta. At 20% net profit (what the college instructor told Ken he could make), he could pay off his college debt within six months of graduation. I guess it all seemed plausible so far.

When I met Ken, he was running out of cash, fast. The first two draws were on time, and he trusted his crew because he was doing the work himself with three buddies he had known for years. But here he was eight weeks into the project, and the bank was pushing back on his next draw against the construction loan.

Ken did not have a job costing system or a budget; he never got around to doing a Gantt chart on the job or writing up a budget for progress billing. How he ever got the construction loan in the first place, I do not know. Maybe his mom helped with that, too.

Ken was in trouble. He had let his costs get out of control and did not even know it. But the banker could see it clear as day. One of my best bookkeepers had to spend over 20 hours to retroactively figure out his job cost, write up a Gantt chart on the project, and match the money from the construction loan to the materials and labor cost. Of course, it did not help that he was paying himself and his three buddies handsomely as they went along.

It then took me three meetings with the bank to convince them to let Ken finish the job. I believe the only reason they agreed was that I was the CFO for other contractors the loan officer knew. Plus, one more thing, Ken's mom had a lot of money on deposit at that bank.

When Ken finished the job, he barely broke even. He did not pay off his college loans, but he learned what the instructors taught when he skipped class. You know, the old school of hard knocks.

During the next four months, it took to complete the house; Wel set up proper job costing and budgeting procedures for Ken. I also sat him down and explained why he should keep using these systems or quit being a contractor and sell cars or something.

I explained to Ken that suitable job costing had three benefits, and the task was not optional if he wanted to keep building.

1. With job costing in place, you can fix errors before it is too late. By comparing the actual cost to the estimates, you can adjust. In the future, when you have crews working, you can use this type of budget so the team knows if they are doing the right job.

2. Every business needs systems to get the work done. If costs are out of line, it is probably because your systems and processes need improvements. Your crews will use the budget to become better at delivering on time and on the money.

3. When you know your total cost by the job, you see where you can better estimate future projects.

A CFO experienced in construction will bring best-in-class solutions to project management, budgeting, job costing, and estimating. It also brings a high level of credibility with vendors and lenders.

Can You Lose Another $50,000 a Year by Missing Change Orders, Upgrades, and Extra Services?

Kevin owns a local remodeling company that has done well over the past few years.

Kevin will tell you it is because he focuses on the NPS score and makes sure he interviews all the customers after the crew has collected the final invoice, cleaned up the job site, and gone home for the weekend. That little extra effort gives him a chance to manage his crews better, but the bigger deal is more referrals from the high-scoring NPS promoters.

Before going to the customer's home, Kevin goes over the project board, the financial reports for that job, and pictures of the new kitchen.

In one case, it was a big job. The customer had spent almost $100,000 to build the kitchen of their dreams. Other than being a 'bigger job,' it all looked normal to Kevin, and he was hoping to get a 90-second video from the customer to post on the company website.

Kevin got his video, but he also got a surprise. The homeowner did an excellent endorsement video talking about the skilled team and how nice the kitchen looked. She continued on about how happy she was that the crew could put in a 60-inch Viking range; after seeing the smaller 36-inch stove.

She praised the crew for re-cutting the cabinets and ordering the bigger gas range; she was one happy camper. But Kevin went over the contract before driving out, and he realized the customer had made some significant change orders mid-stream, and he did not see an invoice for those upgrades.

Kevin was good enough at human engineering to keep his mouth shut and not say anything out of haste without details. But when he arrived at the shop, he ran some numbers and realized his foreman had failed to bill for the extras.

The foreman did not get fired on Monday morning, but he learned about using the billing process we created. When we started the CFO job with Kevin, we installed a phone app the field crews used to take pictures and record events. The complete file went to the bookkeeper to make sure the company was billing for everything they did.

Now Kevin had a problem. He needed to bill the customer $11,500 for the change order, and they were not expecting it. The foreman cannot remember if he told the customer the 60-inch Viking range would cost more or that cutting new kitchen cabinets and countertops might add to the total labor cost.

Beyond the money, Kevin was thinking how he could lose a happy customer along with the repeat and referral business they would bring in over the next ten years. But that $11,500 would come right out of his kids' college fund if he did not fix this.

Kevin had read Robert Cialdini's book Influence: The Psychology of Persuasion, so he had some ideas on keeping the customer happy. But he knew getting his $11,500 while keeping the customer happy was going to be dicey.

By the way, if you have not read Cialdinis' book, I recommend you go to Amazon right now and order it. You will learn how to persuade people to take your bid over the competition, how to get your employees to get behind your vision, and how to generate a lot more leads from your high NPS score customers. Well worth the few hours reading and twenty bucks.

Kevin decided he first had to get the customer to commit to the value of the work. Commitment leads to consistency, the number two principle in Cialdini's book.

Kevin also had to get some type of public commitment, so the customer had a reputation to uphold. Humans want to be consistent. If they say something, especially in public, they want to look like they stick to their word.

I know most of us would have bulldozed an invoice out and got angry with the customer if we got pushback, but Kevin wanted to keep this customer in the promoter column.

Here are the steps he took:

1. He sent a thank-you note, handwritten, with the last sentence: "It is always a pleasure to deal with kind and honest homeowners. My crew said you were some of the nicest people they had worked with in years." Kevin was giving the customer a reputation as a nice person.

2. That evening, Kevin posted the 90 seconds recorded in the kitchen to the company website and sent the customer a link to thank them again for the chance to build their dream kitchen.

3. Kevin then posted the video to the customer's social media pages and asked the customer to share – which she did because she loved the kitchen so much.

It took five days to complete. It was 100% honest. The customer loved the kitchen; she loved the contractor, and she wanted to tell everyone she knew about her new stove.

Now came the dicey part. Kevin wrote the customer a letter (do not use email for this type of thing, put a stamp on it) that he was wrapping up the paperwork and could not find the invoice for the upgrade on the stove.

He would keep looking for it and get back to the customer in a day or two. The soft advanced notice gave the customer a chance to think about the event and realize they would probably receive another bill without being put into an embarrassing situation or suffering from sticker shock without warning.

Two days later, Keven called and said, "I just got off the phone with your friend Jill; she liked your kitchen video and wants to talk to us about remodeling hers. That is excellent news, and I wanted to thank you. Oh, by the way, can I stop by at 6 PM for a few minutes with the updates on the stove?"

Kevin got lucky with the friend, validating the public commitment. But even without the referral, this was going to work. When Kevin stopped by, he brought out the contract and job specs; after a little southern hospitality small talk about the job, he mentioned they did not include the cabinet changes and the stove upgrade. Those were add ons, and here was the invoice.

At this point, the customer had emotionally invested herself in the kitchen and had endorsed the contractor publicly on video. Plus, her friend was now negotiating a kitchen of her own. So, she only grimaced a little and wrote the check.

This event had little to do with the CFO's job. But I wanted to share it with you because, without our advisory role in these types of problems, Kevin would have fired up his D9 bulldozer and plowed the customer relationship under a mountain.

With a CFO on board, problems like change orders, upgrades, and expanding the scope of work do not become a crisis. Your CFO will train your team on how to record money movement in the field when it happens to ensure the complete details land on the bookkeeper's desk in moments. That is the end of missed billing.

Summary

Implement job costing and project management immediately. When running one or two jobs, you can remember everything you're doing with a notepad. Once you have a team in place, you need systems to track the cost of every job in real-time. Job costing always pays for itself with better controls on cash flow and production.

CHAPTER 12:
BAD BOOKKEEPING
CAN PUT YOU OUT OF
BUSINESS FAST.

About fifteen years ago, a contractor fired me from a CFO engagement because he did not like what we found when digging into his business. He thought we were crazy when we made some extensive recommendations in the first ten days on the job that would turn the business upside down.

Sometimes we are so emotionally anchored to bad employees, services that we do not do well, and even business-killer customers from hell that we cannot make logical changes or improvements. Psychologists call this the fallacy of the "'sunken-cost." We have so much invested in a bad project or person who, no matter how much evidence we see, we reject writing it off and getting the chaos out of our life.

"John" had a business doing around $1 million a year installing hardwood floors in new home and office construction. No matter how hard John worked, or how much he invested in better equipment or paid top dollar for the best installers, he was going nowhere year after year.

John was thankful that he had one general contractor who sent over $500,000 of business every year. If not for his best customer, he would never make all the loan payments he had on equipment or keep his installers on payroll year-round.

When we started working with him, the first thing we found was that John had managed his poor cash flow by cutting bookkeeping costs. The only problem with that decision was John had no idea what was going on in his business, and he had no hope of finding out why he worked 60 hours a week, and his family still had to depend on his wife's income to make the rent.

It seemed logical that we should do retroactive job costing and budgeting if we had to clean up the mess, starting with the biggest customer jobs first and working our way down. John was not going broke because of a $4,000 job; something bigger was going on. So we started with the $500,000 a year customer.

When we dug in and started analyzing the numbers on his customers, we had a few questions about "Mr. Big" right out of the gate.

- Does this client ask you for discounts?
- Does he push you to expand the scope of the jobs once you are out there but does not want to pay more?
- Has he ever asked you to drop everything and give him a rush job?
- Are the job sites open and ready to go when you arrive, or do you ever get stuck waiting?
- Does he demand specific installers – causing you scheduling chaos?

- What about his payment history - are your invoices cleared up on the day they are due?

- Has he referred you to other generals who might spend $500,000 a year as well?

As you might imagine, the meeting did not go well.

When John looked at my list of questions, he got antsy at first, then downright angry. Since I had little sales or persuasion skills at that point (remember, accountants are not known for their sales skills), I probably handled this meeting poorly.

I blurted out that this was John's fault for cutting back on bookkeeping. I explained point-blank that Mr. Big was paying John $500,000 a year, but it looked like it cost him $600,000 a year to deliver. I told John he should be grateful for the $4,000 jobs because if he did not have the little guys at a profit, he would have gone bankrupt a year ago.

When he calmed down a little, I told him, "You need to fire Mr. Big today, walk off the jobs in progress, and demand a renegotiation of all your contracts." John's reply was, "Without that $500,000, how will I make payroll on the installers?"

It may have been my burst of laughter that caused me to get thrown out. John did not realize that without Mr. Big, he would not have to make as much payroll, and he would be better off. John fired me on the spot.

The story ends as you would expect. I kept tabs on John, and he closed the doors in late December. I called another client in floor installation and told him to drive out to John's house on Christmas eve and make a deal to buy his equipment, phone number, tradesmen roster, and his customer list for a dime on the dollar. It worked. John was desperate and took the envelope of cash that we had recommended. At least John's kids got a Christmas.

The first thing my other client did was go to Mr. Big and tell him, "This is why John went out of business – if you want me to take over, this list of problems will not happen." Mr. Big laughed and said, 'Okay.' Mr. Big knew he was killing John and did not care. I recommended to my other client that they put a short leash on Mr. Big, or he would figure out how to kill you, too. Bad customers cause chaos wherever they go.

John closed the doors, and my other client hit $2-million the following year. By the way, Mr. Big is off making someone else's life miserable; my client fired him a few months later. Good riddance.

To this day, I am sorry that I did not soften my advice to John. I should have given him the management reports and let him come to his own conclusion, one he would not have defended because of the 'sunken cost' fallacy. Today I would have brought the banker into the meeting to help me explain the problems I discovered. Today, I am better at human engineering, and I tell all my CFO clients that they must learn sales skills even if they are production managers. In business, we are always selling, so you get good at it.

I told you this story because every contractor I've seen fail has looked at bookkeeping as a waste of money. So they let their wife do the books or hired the cheapest bookkeeper they could find.

HUMAN ENGINEERING TIP: The most successful contractors have trained themselves to understand humans. Every dollar that comes in or goes out is moving because someone wants something. If you learn how to understand and motivate your customers, employees, and vendors, your life will be a lot more fun.

What will you get out of good bookkeeping?

At the beginning of this book, you learned that the most important strategic decision you can make in your business is to profile your ideal "good client" and then put your energy into finding more customers that match that profile.

You learned that 20% of the customers drive 80% of the net profit in business, and the rest is only noise and chaos. But we also tend to keep bad customers because we need the cash flow to support our overhead.

After selecting the best client profile, your next step is to pick out the type of build you want to become famous for doing better than any competitors.

Using the 80/20 rule to focus on your best 20% becomes difficult if your bookkeeping is inaccurate. That is because you are unsure who is driving profit and who is driving busy work. It is easy to tell who spends the most money, but net income is a long way from gross sales.

Good numbers that you can trust will lead you to an easier road to prosperity.

We will not make any rash recommendations on bookkeeping in the first few weeks of working for you, and we need to discover what you have in your accounting before we have any advice. However, you have a couple of options if the books are failing you. The first one would be to upgrade your bookkeeping position. The downside is qualified employees are hard to hire in today's business environment.

So the second option is to outsource the entire bookkeeping function. Most people don't realize this, but 80% of the Fortune 500 have turned their entire accounting department over to one big eight accounting firms. The biggest reason is that technology today makes in-house bookkeeping far too expensive. You get better numbers for less money when you use someone who knows how construction accounting works.

Will I Recommend Outsourced Bookkeeping to You?

One of the first places the CFO can cut your cost is bookkeeping. This one step alone may end up covering the investment of a part-time CFO. Our firm does the entire bookkeeping for other contractors from our office, but it may not be suitable for you. We do not need to do the books to get our help as your finance department.

If you have dumped the books on your wife and she is unskilled, believe me, she will be ecstatic if you take the job back. Remember Sam, who you met at the beginning of this book. He realized that bookkeeping saved him more money than it cost.

If you have a crackerjack bookkeeper – keep them, and we will work arm-in-arm. They will probably be relieved because every bookkeeper has questions that need an accountant's point of experience on coding transactions, missing data, or the next government regulation.

However, if you have doubts about your current numbers, do not let your "sunken-cost" emotions decide for you. Poor bookkeeping is the most common root cause of the number one mistake: "I waited too long to ____" and the sin of the inaccurate assumption. Waiting too long to fix problems has bankrupted more contractors than any other single cause.

You will know if this is happening if you have found so many errors in the books that you quit using them to manage the budget on a specific project. If you are looking at the jobs board and then checking online to see how much cash you have in the bank today, you are already on thin ice. Not using the books is a red flag that a CFO would not tolerate.

But bookkeeping is not cheap, and there are costs associated with the task that we never seem to understand as contractors.

First, what you pay the bookkeeper is not the total cost of ownership. Paying $20 an hour can draw up to $50 an hour in total cost. The bookkeeper gets benefits and takes up office space a salesman could use. Add in the employment taxes and computers and software and training to use them. On top of that, you need to add in your time to manage them.

Worse, lousy bookkeeping costs you at tax time as the books have to be fixed, and in many cases, you lose tax deductions because of inadequate record-keeping.

It is easy to run "cost of ownership" reports from your accounting software and show the $50 number. The bottom line is if you have a full-time bookkeeper, you are probably sinking $70,000 to $100,000 in total overhead allocation and payroll to the function. That is no longer necessary with today's technology.

But the costs go even higher. Every employee you hire brings drama, and bookkeepers seem to be a little more dramatic than most. You will listen to family problems and kid problems every week, and you will never know if they will show up because of a school play or the flu that is going around.

Please let me repeat myself here, if you have a good bookkeeper, by all means, keep them? If you don't trust your accounting software, you need to make some changes.

Help Is On The Way

As your CFO, we will bring best-in-class tech to your business, allowing you to upgrade the way you do some of your workflows, but the changes will be for the better.

With today's technology, we can do your bookkeeping from our office for a lot less than your current cost of ownership for the function. We use the online technology to capture invoices from vendors, downloads from the credit card company, and change orders from the field – all electronically. That means you will drop tens of thousands a year to the bottom line, starting almost immediately.

The most significant difference you will notice is that instead of walking into the bookkeeper's office, you will text questions and requests to our office in real-time. But that will not happen often. A well-run business does not need crisis management. Within a few months, you may never need to talk to the bookkeeper again. With the bookkeeping desk empty, we should talk about putting a salesman in that space. Instead of the room being a black hole for cash flow, let's make it a revenue center.

What I hope would happen is that we save you so much money on bookkeeping, wasted overhead, run-away expenses, and low bids for the wrong customer that our CFO services don't cost you a dime. You would start using a dashboard like the sample I posted earlier in this book, and you would talk to me every week about cash flow and profits and how to improve both with a few minor improvements every week.

Remember, you only have to do things 1% better each month to build a 2-million dollar business in a few years.

Bookkeeping is optional, but it should be part of our discussion.

Compliance and Regulations

Waking up at 3:00 AM worrying if you filed the sales tax report on time or made the 941 deposit (payroll taxes) is nuts. If you have ever had a failure in this area, it starts small, but the pain seems to keep getting bigger – it is a domino effect. That is chaos you do not need.

Even if you have a bookkeeper taking care of it, they can miss a compliance deadline or fail to tell you about new insurance regulations for employees driving company trucks. The worse that happens for these critical mistakes is the bookkeeper gets fired. But you get stuck with the bill.

As your CFO, we have a license and insurance. We have a fiduciary responsibility to make sure nothing falls through the cracks to put your business at risk. Most of this is only a check box and fill-in-the-blank work, but it is comfortable at 3 AM to know we have your back.

Tax Planning and Filing

When Donald Trump starts any project, tax people are in the room, sitting right next to the architect and the local traffic control advisor. Trump is planning his tax bill before he plans on what the building will look like. But remember, he is a billionaire, so he has several options for reducing the government's take.

What I find amusing is that the tax guy has a second job to find out what kind of government subsidies and low-interest loan guarantees might be available for big projects like this. So, not only is Trump planning to pay the least in taxes, but he is also using other people's taxes to reduce his upfront risk. You have got to love billionaires.

I do not blame Trump. He always said they rigged the system, and he would be foolish not to use what everyone else on Park Avenue used. Trying to change that system did not work out for him.

By the way, it is the job of your CFO to find and qualify for government largesse if something comes up for the little guy in Atlanta. We will stay on top of it.

For a corporation and the owner, there are eighty-four legal strategies to reduce your taxes. But only a dozen are even close to being set up for a small contractor. For the contractor netting around six figures, your options are limited.

Now you may have already done this, but the first tax strategy is to get out of being a sole proprietor and start some form of a corporation. That reduces your liability exposure and reduces self-employment taxes. There is also a changing list of tax credits you might be eligible for, and you need to plan for those credits now if you want the refund check next year.

Of course, we will set up a 401 (k), so you are scraping money right off the top and into your retirement. You could hire your kids for $12,500 a year and let them pay for their own tuition. It is probably feasible to rent your house out to your corporation fourteen days a year to hold company meetings. If you must buy heavy equipment, we may want to set up a second "leasing" corporation to rent the equipment out to yourself.

Generally, we can move around 25% of what you make off your 1040 with a half dozen strategies for small contractors. When you start making 20% off $2-million, and we have time to plan, we have more legal tax reduction steps that we'll review.

Tax reduction for a contractor is something that I work on every week. However, if you believe you can reduce your taxes on April 14th – you are in for some bad news. Tax reduction is a 12-month-a-year planning process, and retroactive "fixes" to reduce your income will fail or get disallowed by the auditor.

We can help you take advantage of every credit, deduction, and deferral we can find, and you will stay legal. I don't want you up at night worrying about getting a letter from the IRS.

Will you get audited?

Yes, someday, and no matter how clever you think you are, 10,000 other guys have tried the same tricks you may think of, and the IRS can see scheming from a mile away. Even worse, when the auditor catches something, they will look back a minimum of three years (possibly every tax return you ever filed if they smell fraud) to see if you pulled that stunt last year as well.

When you get caught (and eventually everyone gets caught), it will lead to gigantic tax bills, and the interest and penalties can exceed your total income for the year. If you are making $175,000 a year, and you get nailed with a $175,000 tax bill – you have some explaining to do when you get home.

Three More Reasons to Show Income

First, it is easier to borrow money if you can show you can make the payments based on last year's income.

Second, some buyers of construction have rules on the size of business they can let bids to. If that limit is "no one under $1 million in revenue last year," and you came in at $950,000 because you sidelined income, that is a foolish way to run a business.

Third, you will pay the penalty for not reporting all your income when you sell your company. If you are doing legal tax planning, you can show you made money and where the money went. But when you are scheming, you cannot admit to anything.

"Thomas" was not a client of mine, but I knew him well. He would not hire me to be his CFO or his tax strategist because he knew how I felt about the old sleight-of-hand maneuvers at tax time, which ended up costing him dearly.

Thomas was proud every time he hid $100 of income – figuring it saved him $20 or $25 in taxes. But since he now considered his booty to be free money, he would spend it unwisely on cars and boats. Assets that go down in value. If he felt good about the $100, he would have invested it. I guess it's just human nature, but he never got ahead with the skimmed money.

I'm not even sure he ever got a good night's sleep worrying that someday he would get caught.

But the big hit came the following year, Thomas decided to sell his business, and the buyer was willing to pay 5x average net profit, but the buyer wouldn't pay for profit that did not show up on the books or in the tax return.

No matter how many times and ways Thomas talked about "off the books" income, the buyer shrugged and said nope. I am surprised the buyer did not walk away. If there are nefarious dealings in one business area, there is a good chance the owner was cutting corners somewhere else. Cutting corners can often mean hidden liability for a business buyer, and they generally pass on deals when they smell a dead rat.

The bottom line was for every $100 that Thomas hid, he reduced his sale price by $500 – all to save $25 in taxes.

My point is simple: you will be far better off with tax planning because you'll have higher business valuations and more money in your pension.

> **HUMAN ENGINEERING TIP:** Can you imagine the mafia guys back in the '30s who built a bridge with inferior concrete to shave a few bucks off the deal? I cannot believe they ever let their kids drive over that bridge, and I bet they went forty years without a good night's sleep worrying about the bridge coming down. What kind of life is that? All for a few more bucks, money long spent and forgotten.
>
> Well, skimming on your taxes is worse because the bridge will fall when you least expect it. The IRS is going to drop a letter on you. Tax problems are not bad at first, but they seem to escalate as they go along. You can end up paying tens if not hundreds of thousands of dollars, lose your house and business (like the steel building erector did), or worse – go to jail.
>
> A good CFO works to mitigate future risks. But when something goes wrong, they have a plan to get you through it.

Taxes Are Not the Problem

Since we have done tax returns for contractors for over twenty years, I have a funny story to tell that you may find offensive.

I cannot tell you how many times a guy comes into my office with $75,000 in net income and wants to know how to do tax planning, so he could get out of the $9,000 he owes. I always laugh because I think, 'Dude, you do not have a tax problem; you have a net income problem.'

I will warn you that $9,000 will probably be the smallest tax bill you ever have in the future. We will plan it down, but you are going to pay because you are going to earn.

No one enjoys sending money to the government. To make it easier to swallow, I just look at my tax bill as a franchise fee so I can do business under contract law. No, it doesn't make it any easier to cut the check, but I think it's funny.

Your aim as a business owner is to build stakeholder value. While you are stakeholder number one, you have an obligation to your family, employees, vendors, and customers. You're first, but they had better get what they need from your business, or they will take remedial action that you may not like.

The point here is that other wealthy contractors who came before you spent their energy filling the stakeholders' needs, hired competent people to manage the compliance and regulations, and focused on building something great. They put their soul where it counted: in creating 100 delighted customers.

I will do what is legal and realistic on your taxes – you drive us to $2-million in revenue and sleep softly tonight.

THE NEXT STEP

After reading this book, I hope you realize that being a rugged individualist, no matter how southern that sounds, means you cannot get much bigger than you already are. Or, as Jack Nicholson once said, "Maybe this is as good as it gets."

However, if you want the income and lifestyle of a bigger and better run business, it is yours for the asking. The sales are out there; you only need to be ready to manage it, which takes a team.

To take advantage of the building boom, you must start with good numbers and make wise decisions based on those numbers. Taking on more jobs without being in control of what you are currently doing will not solve your problems; it will only increase your current headaches.

Having a second set of eyes on your business helps ensure you see the truth and not fall for the fallacy of the 'sunken cost' or commit the 'sin of the inaccurate assumption' or worse, end up saying 'I waited too long to _____.'

In history, every successful business owner has built a core group of people they can depend on for honest and thoughtful advice. Your CFO should be number one on the list.

Even more important, the CFO knows the secret to your current success. They can figure out the 80/20 rule using real numbers, not hope. The CFO knows the foundation of your long-term growth is in your current accounting. You have already done many things right, or you would not have made it this far.

The bottom line: Have good numbers, so you do not make mistakes. Have advisors, so you do not need to do everything yourself.

A CFO will start with four projects.

- What customer type fits your high-profit profile?

- What type of project is the most profitable for you?

- Drastically slash your expenses by reducing any spending that does not directly impact your customers' experience.

- Set up systems to catch cash leakage.

Doing these first four steps will improve cash flow immediately, and you are going to win bigger bids because you are targeting your best projects and best customers. You will see improvements in as little as a few weeks.

When you take these four strategic steps, you will, on average, increase your net cash flow by around 25%. In the long run, the impact will be even higher.

I have learned from other contractors that it is easy to feel overwhelmed by the important steps of building a business. Most contractors should drive big red trucks because it seems they spend their days putting out fires.

You will only get these first four foundation steps done is to get someone in there as the moneyman who understands your industry and goals. Someone you can depend on to be standing right behind you along the way. A part-time CFO is not an expense; it is an investment that pays out quickly, especially if we can find enough waste and missed billing to cover the cost.

How much money does it take to get a part-time CFO?

Well, once again, hopefully, nothing in the long run. A good CFO will find missed billing opportunities, cash leakage, and overpaid taxes in the first round. The cash savings should cover our costs almost immediately.

On average, you can expect to pay a part-time CFO between $250 and $1,000 per week. Interestingly, most contractors start somewhere in the middle of that range and quickly ask us to do more as they see the results on their bottom line. Of course, it will take a lot longer to implement the changes we have talked about at the lower end price range because I cannot do as much work.

What is the first step in finding out if we can help you get to two million and then beyond?

Generally, we like to have a quick phone call, or even better, a short Zoom meeting. In that meeting, we will start with the question, "what would change in your life if your business was bringing in two million a year and dropping $400,000 to the bottom line?"

Are those changes important enough to you to take on the challenges of building a bigger and better business?

My follow-up questions will include:

1. What dangers do you face in the future that keep you up at night?

2. What opportunities are getting away from you?

3. Where are your strengths? What do you feel you do better than most contractors out there?

Now, these are easy and low-risk questions, but it will give both of us a chance to start building a plan. If we like each other on our first call, we will move to a personal meeting. There will be no billing for the call or the meeting; we are still trying to figure out if I can help and if you want the help.

So, in our first meeting, I will bring a big 3-ring binder with me. This will be the framework of the business plan we will use to help you get to two million. Even if we do not work together, you may keep the plan, and it will guide you in moving forward in the future.

In our first meeting, I will gift you the business plan I use to help other contractors.

The reason I lay out the two-million-dollar firm plans is to help you understand the many planning tasks and decisions that larger contractors have already completed to get where they are. The great thing about building a business is that you do not need to figure everything out for yourself, and you can skip the trial and error if you borrow the answers from somebody else.

We have identified the strategic decisions that all larger businesses made in their first few years to get to multi-million-dollar revenue levels. You get that list at our first meeting.

The first chapter of your business plan focuses on where you are today, where you want to be, and what obstacles stand in your way. Once you have given a problem a name, it is already 25% fixed.

The binder will become the foundation for your operations manual on how to run your company. Your goal is to build a business that is system-driven, not founder-driven. As Michael Gerber talked about in the E-myth, focus your energy 'on' your business, not in the business. So, documenting how the finance, marketing, and production parts of your business run, without the owner being involved in every task is critical if you want to get to two million and beyond.

The first four steps (I am repeating myself here) are universal to all our business clients because it is important to us that we do not become a financial burden on your business. The CFO should be a profit center, so we want to get this work done as soon as possible.

- What is the profile of your highest profit customers?

- What type of project is the most profitable for you?

- Where can we drastically slash your expenses by reducing any spending that does not directly impact your customers' experience?

- Set up systems to recapture the cash that is leaking out of your business.

Those first two steps will help you focus on your best work for your best customers, and the second two will help your cash flow.

Then we will

- Review your tax returns to make sure you are not overpaying.

- Analyze your bidding and billing systems to correct future sales that are priced too low.

- Make sure your bookkeeping is accurate and look for ways to cut bookkeeping costs.

- Create reports to let you know the profitability of each job in real-time.

- Develop a budget with good / better / best scenarios to prevent nasty surprises.

- Meet with you weekly or monthly via zoom to review the progress and problems.

From this point, we break the tasks up into the three categories of running any business, finance, production, and marketing. We can solve problems as your growth uncovers the weak spots in your operation from here on out.

Four Point Summary

The most significant impact you can make in your business is to pick what you like to do and stop doing everything else. Stop working with customers that are not fun. Stop paying employees that cause chaos. Stop worrying about details like cash flow. Stop taking every job that comes along.

Then, build a team made up of people of character. You can train technical skills, but you cannot teach honesty, persistence, or a sense of personal responsibility. In our home, we ask about each customer, vendor, and employee we deal with. "Is this someone we would have over for Sunday dinner after church? Would we put this person at the dinner table with our children?" We stop what we dislike doing, and our life is easier.

Plan your future expansion through referrals from happy customers. That starts with the NPS score sheets. You might need to advertise, but I would love to keep it to a minimum.

Keep a tight ship on your operations. Remember, wealthy contractors, spend as much time on spreadsheets as they do plans. Numbers are the foundation of prosperity.

Imagine that for a moment—not a 100-hour, or a 60-hour, or even a 40-hour workweek; instead, imagine working only 30 hours a week—about six hours a day, Monday through Friday. Plus, one three-day weekend each month so you have time to enjoy the money you make with lasting memories with your family.

Think for a moment about the look on your kids' faces when they get to travel with Dad. And think how nice it will be to take four weeks of vacation each year. Will you take them all at once? Will you travel? Where will you go?

Do you have that picture in your mind? Great!

Then I have one last question for you.

Do you want what you see? Do you want it enough to take the first small, easy step right now?

Good

Call me. Let's get the ball rolling for you. Let's get you on the path to $2-million and get you into the 1% by building a business that frees you up instead of stressing you out.

I *want* to work with determined business owners who want a better life and a better business. I *want* to work with "Yes, and ___" people. If you are one, call me and let's talk.

770-459-1051

Or you can find my website and reach me here: go.bottomline. tax/contractors

Either way, I hope to speak with you soon. Today is the best day to get started!

Jemel Smith CFO

Made in United States
Orlando, FL
03 April 2024

45418711R00088